"The Path to CEO :
A Journey of Failure, Resilience, and Growth"

Jung Seong-ouk, as CEO of UTOP Construction and UTOP Group, has played a pivotal role in the growth and development of both the company and the group at large. Under his leadership, UTOP Construction has achieved stable and consistent performance in the construction industry, successfully executing diverse projects domestically and internationally. CEO Jung has continuously implemented strategic management practices to drive the company's growth, while fostering a forward-looking corporate vision aimed at long-term sustainability.

1. Management Philosophy

CEO Jung's approach to management is founded on principles of responsible governance and continuous innovation. He prioritizes customer satisfaction and emphasizes quality and safety as core components of his business philosophy. Thanks to this approach, UTOP Construction has earned a trusted reputation across sectors such as architecture, civil engineering, residential development, and renewable energy.

CEO Jung is also committed to environmentally conscious and sustainable construction, actively adopting eco-friendly technologies and forward-thinking construction methods that align with future industry trends. His goal is to strengthen the company's competitive edge over the long term and to guide UTOP Construction in fulfilling its social responsibility as a progressive, sustainable enterprise.

2. Leadership and Achievements

CEO Jung has been instrumental in building a solid foundation for long-term growth, carefully reinforcing the company's fundamentals. Under his leadership, UTOP Construction has successfully completed numerous large-scale projects, solidifying its market position. With a focus on sound financial management and efficient organizational structures, the company continues to record steady growth year after year.

In addition to leading UTOP Construction, CEO Jung has focused on enhancing interdepartmental cooperation within the group and maximizing synergy across UTOP's subsidiaries. This collaborative approach has bolstered the group's overall competitiveness and ensured a robust operational base, positioning UTOP Group as a leader prepared for continued success and expansion in its sector.

CEO Jung Sung-wook remains dedicated to YUTOP's mission of sustainable growth and industry leadership, with an unwavering commitment to innovation, responsibility, and excellence.

3. Social Responsibility and Corporate Commitment

CEO Jung places high importance on corporate social responsibility (CSR) and actively promotes a variety of initiatives to support and uplift local communities. Under his guidance, UTOP Construction has engaged in numerous social contribution activities that benefit local residents, thus strengthening its role as a community-oriented company. These initiatives have not only enhanced the company's relationship with local communities but have also positively impacted YUTOP's reputation, fostering trust and goodwill within the broader society.

By fostering this mutual support, CEO Jung aims to build UTOP Construction's image as a reliable partner to both its stakeholders and society at large, affirming the company's commitment to sustainable, socially-conscious growth.

4. Future Strategy

CEO Jung actively champions digital innovation and the adoption of smart construction technologies to respond to the evolving landscape of the future construction market. His forward-thinking leadership embraces a long-term vision that aligns with both the present and future of UTOP Construction, positioning the company to achieve sustainable growth amid industry.

Contents

Foreword: The First Step Toward Challenge and Success

Part 1: From Individual to Leader – The Beginning of Self-Development
- Chapter 1: The Importance of Self-Awareness and Goal Setting
- Chapter 2: Building a Mindset for Growth
- Chapter 3: Discovering and Utilizing Strengths

Part 2 : Time Management and Productivity Enhancement
- Chapter 1: Core Principles of Time Management
- Chapter 2: Enhancing Focus and Managing Distractions
- Chapter 3: Designing a Productive Workday

Part 3 Part 3: Self-Management for Goal Achievement
- Chapter 1: Setting and Tracking SMART Goals
- Chapter 2: Building Confidence Through Small Wins
- Chapter 3 : The Power of Persistence and Motivation

Part 4 : The Art of Communication and Trust
- Chapter 1: The Power of Communication – Listening and Feedback
- Chapter 2: Building Trust and Managing Relationships
- Chapter 3: Persuasive Communication Skills: Moving Minds and Inspiring Trust

Part 5 : The Power of Challenge and Overcoming Crisis
- Chapter 1: The Mindset of Turning Crisis into Opportunity
- Chapter 2: The Attitude Toward Failure
- Chapter 3: Succeeding with Tenacity and Patience

Part 6 : Habits for Sustainable Success
- Chapter 1: Small Habits, Big Changes
- Chapter 2: Maintaining Balance Between Work and Life
- Chapter 3: Realignment and Growth After Success

Epilogue: Walking Together on an Endless Journey of Growth

Foreword:
The First Step Toward Challenge and Success

The journey to success does not begin with bold, grand ambitions.

It doesn't begin with dazzling or lofty goals. Instead, it starts in quiet moments, within small, unassuming decisions and humble habits. When people speak of success, they often picture grand achievements and rapid transformations. But true success emerges only when those small steps accumulate and eventually alter the course of our lives in ways we could never have foreseen.

The story I want to share in this book is precisely about those modest habits and the steady pursuit of self-improvement. I, too, began with a vague dream, though at first, it felt distant and intangible, like something I could only glimpse from afar. I had a strong desire to accomplish something, but I didn't know where to begin. It was in those uncertain moments that I found my way forward, one small action at a time. Gradually, my days began to shift through seemingly minor routines—setting brief plans each morning before work and taking a few moments each evening to reflect on the day.

"Today, I'll move forward, even just a little." With that daily pledge to myself, a shift began each morning as I set out on my commute. During the quiet moments—over coffee, at my desk, reviewing the day's objectives—I would steady my thoughts and ground myself in purpose. I wrote down my intentions for the day each morning, and each evening, I reflected on my progress. Slowly, my approach to work and my mindset began to change.

The Significance of Small Successes, Small Achievements

Great results did not arrive instantly. But over time, I noticed subtle changes in myself as small successes accumulated. Each day, that brief morning session to organize tasks and the quiet moments of evening reflection shifted something in me, almost imperceptibly.

Small victories, often hidden in overlooked moments, had a profound impact. People sometimes dismiss small tasks as insignificant, yet great achievements grow from these humble successes. The sense of accomplishment from even the smallest completed task nudged me forward, little by little. This process of building upon small successes is, in truth, what eventually transforms our lives.

These modest achievements gradually reshaped me and, before I realized it, had altered the course of my life. Each day, those small steps piled up, forming a solid foundation for larger ambitions and goals to follow. This quiet power—the force of steady, cumulative progress—is what I wish to share with you. It is the story that begins here, with these pages.

Valuable Lessons Gained Through Failure

The most profound lessons in life often come not from success but from failure. While many people dread failure and seek to avoid it, the truths we uncover in our moments of defeat hold unparalleled value. I, too, have faced many setbacks. During my first major project, I encountered a series of mistakes and budget overruns that seemed insurmountable, leaving me plagued by a sense of helplessness and despair for some time.

Yet, as that difficult period passed, I realized that it was those failures that ultimately transformed my life. In revisiting the site of my missteps, I found myself reflecting deeply on my approach and my choices. Failure had not knocked me down; rather, it opened up new paths, allowing me to seek better solutions. Pushing through the pain of failure, I began to refine my methods, and, over time, the small victories that followed accumulated into tangible success.

Failure gave me the chance to find a better direction. Without these difficult experiences, perhaps the success that came later would never have been possible. As I will share throughout this book, it is through repeated failures that we learn, adapt, and ultimately grow. Failure has proven to be a stepping stone to genuine growth. I hope that my own journey through setbacks can help readers understand that every failure is the start of something new.

A Space for Happiness, Success for Happiness

If the ultimate purpose of success is happiness, then what kind of life should we be striving for? For me, true happiness has been about creating spaces where people can live, where they can spend time with family and find moments of peace.

Creating places that hold life's most cherished memories has given me a deep sense of responsibility and fulfillment. The value of my work lies in the small, everyday moments that bring happiness to others. If someone can laugh freely, rest comfortably, or gather with loved ones in these spaces, then I, too, find my own happiness there.

The Value of Success Shared with Employees

As I managed the company, I realized that success is never something achieved alone. Along the path to every accomplishment were the dedication and hard work of colleagues and employees. One of my most important goals, therefore, has always been to create an environment where each person feels pride and a sense of fulfillment in their role. When employees grow, and through their growth, the company as a whole advances—I have come to believe that this is the true engine of success.

Watching employees immerse themselves in their work, achieving results with steadfast dedication, taught me a valuable lesson: they, too, strive every day to improve, even if only a little. Their small achievements, their resilience, have always been a source of strength for me. I believe it is my role as a leader to provide them with a supportive work environment and spaces for open communication, so they can continue to grow.

When the growth of the company aids employees in their personal growth, and when employees' happiness aligns with the organization's goals, that is when true success is achieved. In this book, I share how I sought to build trust with my employees as a leader, and how I encouraged their growth along the way. I am convinced that the most meaningful achievements are those that we experience together, growing and succeeding side by side.

May This Book Be Your First Step

This book encapsulates my journey of challenges and triumphs. There were moments filled with hope and passion, and other times when I walked alone, standing firm in the face of failure. Along that path, I made countless promises to myself and followed them, one step at a time. It was these promises, steadily building upon each other, that guided me forward. I hope this book brings a spark to your own journey.

Life's transformations rarely come from grand events. Brilliant successes and visible accomplishments take root in the quiet routines of daily life. Yet, as we move through each day, we often forget the significance of those small steps. Sometimes, today's efforts may feel meaningless, and we may lose sight of why we work so hard. At those times, I hope this book can be a source of renewed strength and courage. Trust that today's small step has the potential to eventually reshape your life.

This book is not just my story; it is the story of all of us. It is a journey of growth, of ordinary people striving to create a better tomorrow. May each page resonate with your own challenges and experiences. The new paths discovered through failure and setbacks may guide you through similar experiences toward greater success and happiness.

As I learned through my own challenges, I hope this book encourages you to reflect within and prepare for the small transformations of tomorrow. May today's single step lead you toward a brighter tomorrow. And may this book become a first step toward that change in your life.

Part 1: From Individual to Leader – The Beginning of Self-Development

Chapter 1: The Importance of Self-Awareness and Goal Setting

The journey toward success begins the moment you truly face yourself. Self-awareness and goal setting are the first essential steps on this path. While each person's path to success is unique, one universal principle remains: thorough understanding of oneself and realistic goal setting are fundamental. Self-awareness allows us to precisely recognize where we stand and what we are capable of. Without this process, no matter how skilled we are, it becomes difficult to take that crucial first step forward.

For me, this became evident when I pursued the Construction Professional Engineer certification in South Korea—a qualification that thousands of construction professionals strive for each year, yet only a few attain. What I learned throughout this journey went far beyond technical skills; it underscored the importance of self-reflection and purposeful goal setting.

The Stage of Self-Awareness on the Road to Success

Self-awareness is the first stage in any journey toward success. It goes beyond simply identifying strengths and weaknesses; it involves clearly understanding one's current position and the areas that need improvement. Many people, when setting goals, focus on desired results or outcomes. Yet, the truly crucial first question to ask oneself is, "Where am I right now?" Only by objectively acknowledging our current abilities and limitations can we gain clarity on the efforts needed to move forward from that point.

The process of self-awareness generally involves the following steps:

1. A Thorough Assessment of Strengths and Weaknesses
Many people are well aware of their strengths, yet often fail to recognize their weaknesses. However, weaknesses not only hinder growth but can become essential focal points for improvement. Accurately identifying one's weaknesses marks the starting point for growth. For instance, someone might excel in technical skills yet lack communication or teamwork abilities; in such cases, addressing these areas should take priority. Acknowledging weaknesses and working to overcome them helps clarify one's direction toward growth.

2. Establishing Your Current Position to Achieve Goals
Once you have an understanding of where you currently stand, the next step is to set specific goals. Goals are often divided into long-term and short-term objectives, with each complementing the other to enable substantial achievements. Long-term goals provide direction, while short-term goals outline the practical steps needed to reach those objectives.

3. Developing a Growth Plan That Matches Your Current Position

Based on an honest understanding of where you are, you need to create a concrete plan that details the steps required at each stage. To ensure that your ambitions do not remain as vague dreams, a realistic action plan bridging the gap between your current position and your goals is essential. For example, to address a specific weakness, you might dedicate 30 minutes each day to studying relevant materials and then apply that knowledge in real-world tasks.

Starting Small: The Power of Incremental Goals

The most important aspect of goal setting is to begin with small, achievable goals. Many people set lofty ambitions, but large goals can make it difficult to experience immediate satisfaction or progress, often leading to burnout. Breaking down larger objectives into smaller, short-term goals allows for consistent progress and makes each step feel achievable.

Small goals allow us to move forward gradually. The sense of accomplishment from each small achievement accumulates, eventually laying the groundwork for larger ambitions. For example, committing to just ten minutes of self-development each day creates a simple goal to practice daily. These small goals build upon each other, providing visible evidence of growth and paving the way to achieve greater aspirations.

Fundamental Principles of Goal Setting

1. Apply the SMART Principle

Goals should be SMART: Specific, Measurable, Achievable,

Relevant, and Time-bound. For example, rather than setting a vague goal like "I will read a self-development book each day," a SMART goal would be, "I will spend 20 minutes each day reading a self-development book and taking notes." This more structured approach increases the likelihood of success.

2. Remember That Small Goals Lead to Great Achievements

Large goals are ultimately the result of many small goals achieved one by one. Consistently acting on each small goal builds up to create a larger success. As these small goals are met, you gain trust and confidence in yourself, along with the assurance that you can move forward. It's not just about accumulating small wins; it's about building the strength to trust yourself and setting even greater goals.

3. Regular Review and Feedback

After setting a goal, it is essential to schedule regular times to give yourself feedback on your progress. Weekly or monthly, take the time to assess where you stand with your goal, consider whether you are on track, and identify areas for improvement. This cycle of review and feedback transforms your goal from a simple plan into a practical force for personal growth.

As you realize each small goal, your life will gradually begin to shift. If you wish to accomplish something big, start with a small goal. It is the practice of achieving these small goals each day that ultimately leads to the attainment of larger accomplishments.

A Shift in Self-Awareness Through the Construction Professional Engineer Certification

The time I spent preparing for the certification was about much more than studying. Each morning at 7 a.m., I headed to the construction site as usual. The site was always bustling with activity, filled with noise, dust, and the biting wind that I faced all day. By evening, I was exhausted, yet I would faithfully open my books as soon as I got home. My goal of earning the certification, and my small daily commitment of reading, studying, and understanding even just 10 minutes each day, kept me grounded.

It was a small goal—turning a few pages each night after work, making one more step forward each day. The process was harder than expected, and there were many days when I felt my resolve waver. Yet, these small goals proved to be more powerful than I had anticipated. Each time I returned to my studies, I was defeating the doubts of my former self. Slowly, the accumulation of small achievements led to the greater accomplishment of obtaining the certification.

But the certification itself was not the end. What I gained was the ability to view myself honestly, the habit of steady reflection, and the practice of beginning again. With the experience of dedicating even 10 minutes each day to my goal, I found myself growing a little stronger each day. As I continuously achieved small goals, I gained the confidence to set larger ambitions, and I came to truly understand the meaning of persistence and discipline.

In the end, this journey became more than a single accomplishment; it became a foundation for my growth.

The First Step from Employee to Leader: Self-Awareness and Goal Setting

As experience and years accumulate, the importance of self-awareness and goal setting becomes clearer. In the early days of my career, I simply completed tasks as they were assigned, but over time, each goal I set became an essential stepping stone for my personal growth.

Moving beyond the phase of working solely for my own performance, I realized that developing the skills necessary for larger goals was crucial. Especially after stepping into a leadership role, I understood that goal setting had to encompass not only my achievements but also the growth of my team and the advancement of the organization as a whole. This realization—that the entire organization must progress together—led me to set goals that were broader and deeper than mere personal growth.

Goal setting is not just a means to achieve results. It is an essential process for self-improvement and for stepping toward a higher level. As I gradually fulfilled each small goal on my way to becoming a leader, I gained a sense of accomplishment and confidence, slowly building the courage to reach for larger ambitions. Ultimately, through experiences of meaningful success, I realized that the path to achievement truly begins with self-awareness. When we look deeply within ourselves and move step by step toward our goals, success begins to seep into our lives, as if by its own accord. It is in this process—where what once seemed like a distant dream finally becomes tangible—that real success is born.

Self-awareness allows us to consistently reflect on where we stand, while realistic, achievable goals create a concrete path for gradual improvement. A day without goals is a day adrift. Without goals, even small achievements may go unrecognized, and time passes with little meaning. But the sense of accomplishment that arises from achieving even the smallest goal builds confidence, empowering us to pursue greater challenges. Before long, these small successes accumulate, ultimately leading to larger achievements and providing the momentum to pursue even greater aspirations.

In this process, we do not merely achieve personal success; we gradually become people who can contribute to the team and the organization. The small goals and accomplishments I attained began to support the growth of the team and organization and, in turn, led to even greater achievements as a leader. I came to understand that a leader is someone who sets goals not only for themselves but for the growth of their colleagues and the advancement of the organization, then steadily works toward those goals.

Looking back, I realize that the first experiences of failure, along with the journey to obtain the Construction Professional Engineer certification, served as the foundation of self-awareness and goal setting that have propelled my career. Through these experiences, I learned the process of building up small goals until they finally culminated in larger achievements. This journey continues to serve as the foundation upon which I grow, step by step.

True success is not merely in setting grand goals and achieving them. Success is found in the small, incremental changes of each day, and this is where its true power lies. Even the smallest goal, when pursued with consistent effort, becomes a force for transformation. It is through these small steps that we find ourselves growing and ultimately discover that we are changing the very direction of our lives.

Examining ourselves, recognizing weaknesses, and working to overcome them is not glamorous work. There are moments when we must set aside pride in the face of failure and mistake, and there are times when we must stand back up, time and time again. In this process, we come to understand ourselves more deeply, and small resolutions accumulate into significant change. This transformation does not happen overnight but unfolds gradually within the rhythms of our daily lives.

The ten minutes spent reflecting on the day each morning, the few seconds during work when we realign ourselves with our goals—these small moments accumulate, reshaping our lives and directing our steps forward. Small accomplishments are not just individual milestones. They become stepping stones toward greater achievements, steadily building our confidence and guiding us toward becoming our best selves.

True success is the product of countless small steps, steadily adding up until it finally takes shape. May this chapter on self-awareness and goal setting serve as a small compass, guiding you as you begin your own journey.

Chapter 2: Building a Mindset for Growth

The path to success may not be as distant as it seems. Often, it lies hidden within our failures and mistakes. Failure usually comes cloaked in a dark, cold mantle, but if we look closely, within it are the seeds of growth and hidden insights waiting to be uncovered. We must learn to pause and confront the question that failure places before us: "How will I rise again?" The journey of seeking answers to this question is, in itself, the foundation of a growth mindset. An apartment development project set against the vast, barren land of Mongolia offered me such moments of confrontation. Beyond the technical skills and knowledge I'd acquired lay the harsh reality of legal and cultural boundaries, and limitations beyond my control.

The Obstacles and Insights Found in the Mongolian Project

In Mongolia, land ownership is never granted to foreigners; land can only be leased for a hundred years. The land there stands strong and self-reliant, just as its people live by long-standing traditions and unique order. What seemed standard and familiar under Korean laws and procedures felt foreign and out of place there. Realizing this difference was a humbling experience; each time I encountered it, the ground beneath me seemed to fade away, leaving me standing on unstable soil.

The project required countless revisions and adjustments, while timelines stretched indefinitely. I remember staring at the distant mountains from the dust-covered car during those long drives.

Endless exchanges of documents, and debates over the interpretation of each line in the contract, dragged on without an end in sight. In those moments, I learned for the first time what it meant to be helpless, watching my intentions dissolve like grains of sand. There are limits that technical skill and knowledge cannot overcome, and it took me a long time to accept this reality.

Realigning After Failure and Discovering Truths Hidden in Mistakes

Accumulated mistakes and misunderstandings forced me to face my failures directly. Failure was not simply a mark of defeat; it was a quiet voice, asking me, "What will you learn from this? How will you move forward?" Only when I could listen to this question did I realize that failure wasn't merely enveloping me—it could become the force that helped me discover a new path.Every day, as I reassessed the project in Mongolia, I looked for lessons to draw from it. Failure opened my eyes to new perspectives, prompting me to reset my smaller goals. I learned to confront unforeseen obstacles and to seek out the lessons hidden within them. This, I realized, is how a growth mindset begins to take root—through the quiet, persistent realizations that emerge in such moments.

Embracing Local Time and Adapting to the Flow

Time passed, as it always does, carrying a current I hadn't fully understood, much like the wind moving along the river. And I had to accept this current. In this new environment, I felt keenly that knowledge and skill alone were insufficient. Mongolian law, culture, and ways of life confronted me as boundaries, sometimes as walls. They had their own customs, a structure that had flowed long before I arrived. I had to adjust myself to their rhythm. The land in Mongolia did not open itself easily to outsiders.

Consulting legal advisors and relying on local experts, I gradually came to appreciate the flow that I had initially overlooked. In time, this foreign environment began to feel more like my own. Adapting to their established structures became more than just a project requirement; it gave me a sense of belonging, a feeling that I was becoming part of the time that shaped this place.

The Strength to Stand Again: The Quiet Power of Small Achievements

The failures I encountered in Mongolia didn't merely bring me to my knees; they also taught me how to find the strength to stand again. Each small achievement, each minor adjustment, helped me reshape my goals to better align with reality. With each new attempt and small success, I found that the fear of greater failures gradually lessened. The quiet reassurance of small victories, and the confidence they provided, became the rungs of a ladder leading me to new heights. Each apartment that rose on the vast Mongolian land felt like a footprint left by my journey.

As these small achievements accumulated, they fostered a greater confidence, which in turn nurtured a courage that would withstand the next failure. These successes didn't just signify the project's advancement; they became seeds of self-assurance growing slowly within me.

True Lessons and Growth Through Failure

Failure still carried its darkness and sharp edges, but I no longer hid from it. I learned how to find light within that darkness, and from the solitude failure brought, I discovered that true growth quietly blooms. The failures I faced in Mongolia extended beyond that single project; they offered profound insights that influenced my life and work as a whole. Choosing not to fear failure but instead to seek its lessons is, in essence, the core of a growth mindset.

In the challenges that followed, I continued to face failures directly, searching within each one for a new way forward. The confidence I gained from facing failure made me stronger, allowing me to stand firm in the face of future setbacks. The strength drawn from failure became a driving force, guiding me toward new paths and deeper maturity.

Chapter 3: Discovering and Utilizing Strengths

To achieve success, it is essential to identify our unique strengths and adapt them to new environments. Each of us possesses our own invaluable assets, but it takes moments of challenge to truly unlock their potential. During my days building Korean-style apartments on the harsh, cold plains of Mongolia, I came to understand this truth. To reach greater heights, I realized I had to hone my skills and carefully consider how to make them shine in this unfamiliar setting.

Discovering Strengths That Shine in New Environments

The land of Mongolia is a cold, unwelcoming expanse dominated by an unforgiving wind. Its climate, cultural background, and even the expressions and ways of life of its people differed greatly from what I knew in Korea. If my skills and experience as a designer in Korea were to make any lasting impact, I had to take a fresh approach. In a place where winter temperatures could drop as low as -40 degrees Celsius, insulation and heating efficiency were non-negotiable. I realized that my abilities were being tested by the overwhelming forces of nature.

Instead of simply applying the design techniques I had learned in Korea, I had to optimize them for local conditions. This was not just a technical challenge—it was a moment to discover what was truly needed for my strengths to shine. While adapting Korean-style insulation and energy-efficient heating structures to Mongolia's barren land, I learned that strengths are more than just knowledge; they are most powerful when combined with adaptability and openness to change.

The Challenges and Solutions of Construction : Moments to Leverage Strengths

Completing the design didn't mean the challenges were over. Mongolia's unforgiving cold tested me throughout the construction process. Materials were hard to come by, and the schedule was at the mercy of the weather. I could not simply apply the management techniques or material allocation methods I'd learned in Korea. Instead of clinging to familiar methods, I had to modify my plans flexibly, adjusting to the realities of this foreign environment. My construction experience truly shone when I approached challenges with adaptability.

Confidence and Insight from Small Successes

The small successes I achieved in Mongolia were more than mere project milestones; they became opportunities to trust myself. Like the buildings that stood firmly on the barren landscape, each small accomplishment made me feel more grounded. What had initially felt unfamiliar and uncertain now became familiar, and I realized that only when my skills and experience adapted to this new land did true success emerge. Once we had implemented Korean standards of heating efficiency and structural stability, the local clients responded positively, and this initial success became a source of motivation for me and my entire team. I came to understand that strengths are not just tools for achieving results but assets that fuel the courage to pursue the next goal.

The Flexibility and Adaptation Needed to Harness Strengths

Through this experience, I learned that the true power of strengths lies in the flexibility to reconfigure them to suit new environments. Effectively harnessing one's strengths is not simply about applying one's skills and experiences as they are but rather about adapting and optimizing them for the situation at hand. My strength lay in my experience with Korean design and construction, but by reshaping it to fit the severe Mongolian climate and local lifestyles, I discovered new possibilities.

For instance, I reimagined Korean apartment layouts and heating technology to meet the unique climate needs of Mongolia. This was not merely an exercise in technical application; it was about delivering results that aligned with the demands and necessities of the local context. Through this process, I realized that strengths do not merely shine when discovered; they reach their true potential when they are reshaped and optimized for new circumstances.

The Confidence and Conviction Gained from Utilizing Strengths

The Mongolian project gave me the confidence to trust in my own strengths, even in new environments. When the experience I had accumulated in Korea proved effective in Mongolia, I became certain that I could deliver results in any setting. This small success became a stepping stone to even greater goals, filling me with the confidence to believe in myself and the courage to embrace even larger challenges.

In later projects, I continued to seek ways to apply my strengths in ways that suited the unique demands of each environment. These experiences have allowed me to grow with steadiness, even when faced with diverse challenges. The process of leveraging my strengths has deepened my self-belief and led me to rediscover my capabilities. Strengths are not merely proof of competence; they are stepping stones that drive us to grow further.

Discovering and Utilizing Strengths: A New Source of Growth

The process of identifying, optimizing, and utilizing strengths went beyond the success of a single project; it became a wellspring of continuous growth. My experience in Mongolia taught me new insights into how to discover and harness my strengths. Since then, I have been able to confront diverse challenges by constantly revisiting and reshaping my abilities.

Strengths are not merely small proofs of competence. They are a solid foundation, enabling us to face an uncertain future without fear, grounding us as we stand on the brink of new paths. Strengths do not simply shine when they are discovered. They become the true source of growth only when refined to fit new environments and adapted to the demands of changing circumstances.

Part 2: Time Management and Productivity Enhancement

Chapter 1: Core Principles of Time Management

The essence of success is rooted in effective time management. Time is a limited resource, given equally to all, yet what we achieve within its flow depends entirely on our choices. Ultimately, time is the most essential asset that shapes the framework of our lives. Managing time is not just about creating schedules or listing tasks. It is about living each day with intention, contemplating what meaning to infuse into each moment and where to place our priorities. In the year when we had to complete a project before the onset of Mongolia's winter, I learned the true essence of time management.

Battling Against Time and the Pressure of Winter

In Mongolia, winter isn't just a cold, harsh season. The brutal temperatures, which drop as low as -40 degrees Celsius, have the power to freeze everything. For the apartment construction project we were working on, winter was an unyielding deadline. Before the ground froze, we had to complete the foundation work, including excavation. Any delay could mean postponing the project indefinitely. Managing time was akin to waging a battle against the cold; the excavation deadline wasn't simply a line in a schedule but an undeniable weight of reality.

This project challenged us with more than simple scheduling.

Weather, environmental conditions, shortages of materials, and unforeseen factors tested our ability to manage time. No matter how well-planned our schedule was, unexpected weather changes or delays in material supply inevitably arose. We had to compress our tasks into the time we were given and prioritize the most critical tasks first. Time would not adjust to us; we had to adapt to it.

Prioritization and Focus :
The Essence of Time Management

The most vital element of time management is prioritization. In situations where everything seemed equally important, identifying what to focus on was challenging. Without this discernment, no amount of hard work could guarantee the best results. In this project, priorities were determined by both the importance of the tasks and the environmental factors, and these decisions directly impacted our outcomes.

My focus was not on completing a list of tasks each day but rather on how meaningfully I spent my time to accomplish them. At the end of each day, I reviewed the work I had done and set specific goals for the next day. Staying late to reevaluate my plans and create new action steps became a habit that allowed me to manage each day more effectively. Each morning, I started by organizing the most crucial tasks for the day, and this routine filled me with renewed energy.

The Power of Small Goals and the Joy of Achievement

The pressure to complete excavation before winter forced us to reorganize our entire construction schedule. Realizing that time was running out made the process of setting small daily goals even more essential. Small goals were broken down into tangible, daily tasks, and achieving these goals allowed me to discover my capabilities and experience the satisfaction that came with each accomplishment.

For the excavation work, we set specific targets for daily progress, and we worked our hardest to meet those objectives. Splitting limited time into manageable goals each day created a habit that steadily built up results. The accumulation of small successes grew into a larger achievement, and the satisfaction from these accomplishments instilled confidence within me. While meeting today's goal didn't guarantee success tomorrow, it taught me how to use time more effectively.

Efficiency and Responsibility: Bearing the Weight of Time

Successful time management doesn't end with completing a day's tasks efficiently. Managing time is about demonstrating your capabilities daily and embracing your responsibilities. On the Mongolian site, I realized that if I didn't manage time well, the next day's work would be even more difficult, ultimately affecting the project's overall success. Time wasn't simply a passing resource; it was a responsibility placed upon us.

When the weather worsened unexpectedly, plans were disrupted, and if materials were in short supply, the schedule was delayed. In such unpredictable circumstances, staying accountable to daily responsibilities required constantly adjusting our plans and following through. As I confronted new challenges every day while honoring my goals and duties, I learned how to master the flow of time.

Improving Time Management with the SMART Principle

One of the most important principles of time management is the SMART framework: setting goals that are Specific, Measurable, Achievable, Relevant, and Time-bound. Applying this principle meant that each day's tasks became more than just items to complete; they became accomplishments. For example, planning even ten minutes for a specific task and following through allowed me to review my progress and give myself feedback.

SMART goals provided a clear action plan. When goals were well-defined and time-bound, they felt like small achievements. Each morning, I set clear goals, and with each goal I met, I moved closer to greater results. Time management was not just a checklist; it was a commitment to consistent achievement, an ongoing process of fulfilling promises to myself.

Living a Life that Masters Time

On the plains of Mongolia, I learned the art of managing time.

Though time is a resource equally available to all, how we use it depends entirely on our choices. Mastering time is not limited to planning each day and following that plan. It involves maximizing each day, turning it into a foundation for future accomplishments.

Living a life that masters time is not merely a technique for success. When small daily goals accumulate and merge into larger objectives, I found growing confidence in my own potential. Each moment spent proving myself within the confines of time empowered me to pursue even bigger goals.

Chapter 2: Enhancing Focus and Managing Distractions

When I first started in sales, everything felt unfamiliar and unsettling. Each initial meeting in this new environment had no set standards; everything depended solely on my own abilities and focus. The walk towards my first client felt quiet, as if all other senses had disappeared. I was uncertain about how to start the conversation or how to capture their interest, and at every step, anxiety held me captive. To get through these moments, I knew I needed unwavering focus and immersion.

Countless Distractions That Obstruct Focus

The world of sales was not a place where skill and knowledge alone could guarantee success. My workdays in sales were filled with distractions. Each day, I had to meet new clients and achieve the best results within limited time. Reports from my superiors, upcoming appointments, and unread emails all continuously disrupted my focus. Even when I needed to center my attention solely on the client, my mind often wandered to other tasks. These distractions shook not only my work performance but also my confidence in myself.

Yet, I knew I had to find a way to maintain focus amidst these disturbances—to truly listen to my clients and convey my message accurately. Beyond simply hearing them, I needed to read their expressions, respond to their cues, and understand their needs deeply. Immersing all my senses into the conversation, cutting off every surrounding distraction, was essential.

Developing Small Habits to Cultivate Focus: Finding My Own Method

It didn't happen easily from the start. There were many trial-and-error experiences. But over time, I began to discover my own methods for staying immersed. Before meeting a client, I cleared unnecessary documents and equipment from my desk. To prevent mental clutter, I kept my phone as far away as possible. I prepared to immerse myself solely in the client's words and reactions.

I also developed a personal ritual for immersion. Before starting each conversation, I took a few deep breaths and briefly reviewed any background information on the client. This allowed me to focus solely on the person in front of me. This habit, repeated each day, helped me feel more at ease and natural in the field.

Accepting Anxiety and Wandering Thoughts as Part of the Process

Anxiety would inevitably surface during those initial conversations with clients. Unbidden worries and thoughts distracted me. "What if the client doesn't accept this idea?" "Will I be late for my next appointment?" "How should I respond to that email from my manager?" These concerns and intrusive thoughts often led me further away from the moment. My mind's predictions of the client's reaction only heightened my anxiety.

Instead of struggling to eliminate anxiety, I learned to embrace it while remaining immersed in the moment. Anxiety is a feeling that can never be completely erased, so I began by simply acknowledging its presence. Whenever I felt anxious, I would quietly recognize it and practiced looking at it for what it was. As I listened to the client's words, I allowed myself to be aware of the anxiety within me. Gradually, it subsided, and I found myself more focused on the client's words.

Daily Training to Strengthen Focus

Focus and immersion weren't skills developed overnight. Each morning before meeting clients, I outlined my goals and thoughts in a notebook. This routine brought me a sense of stability. Before every meeting, I revisited the client's needs and assessed my role, preparing myself for the conversation. At the end of each day, I reviewed the meetings, noting any missed opportunities and areas for improvement. This process became a small indicator of progress, a routine that helped reduce anxiety and boost my confidence.

I reinforced my focus even outside of work through small practices. I would immerse myself in reading or jot down thoughts that came to mind during a walk, later applying these insights to client interactions. For example, I remembered the calm I felt in nature and took a deep breath before meeting a client, recalling that tranquility when anxiety struck. These habits became my personal focus training.

The Courage and Confidence Built Through Small Successes

As moments of immersion deepened in front of clients, small successes started accumulating. When clients listened closely to me, when their eyes focused on mine, I began to feel the power of my concentration. These small successes brought me immense confidence. With each meeting, I grew more certain that I could improve, and even past failures transformed into experiences that strengthened me.

They began to understand the message I conveyed and recognize the value they sought. Success in sales went beyond figures on a contract. When clients expressed satisfaction, when trust was built, I witnessed the impact of my immersion and focus on real outcomes.

The Focus Nurtured Through Anxiety Became My Own Strength

As time passed, I learned how to manage the anxiety that arose in sales. With each meeting, I discovered a version of myself who remained steady, even amid distractions and uncertainties. Immersion became my way of staying grounded, a support that kept me steady in any environment. In front of clients, I continued to feel both tension and anxiety. Yet, rather than undermining my focus, that anxiety became something I embraced, strengthening my resolve.

Anxiety became a force that propelled my growth. In each encounter, I realigned myself, listening deeply to clients' voices, discerning what they needed. These small moments of immersion gradually built up, providing me with newfound confidence and certainty.

The moments when I could focus fully were found only within the shared space between myself and the client. My immersion was my authentic self before them, and the small successes that emerged from this focus ultimately led me to greater heights.

Chapter 3: Designing a Productive Workday

A successful workday is not merely a sequence of hours arranged on a schedule. For me, each day was like a stage, a space where I refined myself little by little to move closer to my goals. Sales, in particular, demanded constant repetition and adaptation. Each day wasn't just a series of meetings but an encounter with new faces, facing both their expectations and doubts. Success here didn't come from quick words or spontaneous persuasion. What I needed instead was quiet preparation, endless practice, and a serious mental simulation with myself.

From the moment I began my commute, I entered my own world. In my mind, I rehearsed conversations with clients like a never-ending drama. I played out my questions, anticipated their responses, and practiced my reactions over and over. This time spent in simulation marked the start of my workday. As the mornings passed, my confidence grew a little each day. If a client showed doubt at my question, I was already prepared with a response. And in finding those answers, I felt myself going deeper, as though understanding my clients brought me closer to understanding myself.

Small Rituals and the Weight of a Workday

In sales, I often felt like someone gathering grains of sand in a desert, building something brick by brick. Before meeting a client, I performed my own small rituals, visualizing our conversation in advance. Though these moments were calm and quiet, they created a profound internal shift. The repetition brought me a sense of peace and instilled a confidence that steadied me in any situation. By practicing these conversations repeatedly in my mind, each workday began to take on a unique tone.

My small rituals also helped calm the anxiety and nervousness that sometimes filled me. Envisioning various scenarios and preparing for them brought a sense of stability. Imagining first meetings filled with anticipation, visualizing the ups and downs of potential outcomes—this series of preparations acted almost like a ceremony, honing me and establishing an inner balance that kept me steady in any environment. Through this process, I grew not only as a salesperson but as someone who understood myself more deeply.

Confidence Built Through an Efficient Routine

My workday became a framework, a vessel shaped by time, in which I could contain my growth. I filled this vessel day by day, setting schedules and plans. Each workday was not simply an arrangement of time for efficiency and results, but rather a structure of time that allowed me to cultivate myself. Preparing calmly before meeting a client, thinking through every possible scenario, gave me an invaluable sense of confidence. Each morning, I aligned my mind and body through my own rituals and organized an efficient day, establishing a sense of order within.

At first, this routine was challenging. Spending extra time preparing for the day and repeating similar exercises before each client meeting sometimes made me wonder if I was on the right path. But over time, the routine gave me a steady sense of stability, which ultimately made me stronger. The small commitments and plans I set each morning became my foundation, and this foundation enabled me to engage wholeheartedly in each moment that mattered.

The Power of Pre-Meeting Simulations: Preparing for Genuine Encounters

Meeting a client was more than just a conversation. It was a moment where I revealed everything I had prepared, a space that demanded authenticity. This is why I rehearsed countless times in my mind before each meeting, envisioning how they might react and anticipating each question they might ask. The simulation process was essential for me. Though clients never knew, I had already rehearsed many conversations in my mind before standing before them. Through this, I could strengthen my resolve to understand the client and deepen my trust in myself.

Daily practice and mental simulations gifted me a sense of small accomplishment. Even if the clients' questions or reactions differed from my expectations, I remained steady. I had rehearsed countless scenarios, so I adapted my responses to suit them. What mattered most in that first meeting wasn't a perfect answer, but an understanding of and empathy for the client's needs. This mindset was the foundation of my daily preparation, and the confidence I gained through it made me stronger.

Confidence and Fulfillment Built Through Time

Each morning, as I planned my day and set small goals, I made promises to myself. Small commitments wove into the fabric of each day, guiding me forward. This process was slow, and at times felt tedious, yet with each passing day, these promises fortified me. Achieving small goals brought a sense of fulfillment, carrying a power greater than I expected. Each day, I prepared in the same place, performed similar exercises, and slowly built a sense of direction. With each accomplishment, joy inspired me to take on greater challenges.

By preparing and closing each day mindfully, I ensured I wouldn't lose sight of my goals. Designing my time and crafting each day in my own way gradually gave me more control. Initially, repeating the same preparations every morning felt meaningless, but over time, I built a trust in myself through this repetition. With each day's experience, I gained confidence, and that confidence became the force propelling me forward. My sense of order, established through these small achievements, strengthened my resolve.

These small achievements didn't simply provide fleeting satisfaction. Each day's small success fueled my confidence to pursue the next goal. With each day filled entirely in my own way, those accumulated hours became a source of inner strength. The uncertain future no longer felt daunting. In this process of building upon time, the trust and confidence I developed in myself made me stronger.

One day, I realized that those seemingly mundane preparations were no longer just a part of my day—they had become the center that sustained my life. The accomplishments built over time were supporting me. As I shared my prepared words with clients, my confidence was more than just eloquence; it was the evidence of the hours I had steadily built each day. The small achievements within each workday became the foundation for persuading others and believing in myself.

These small successes became part of who I am. The experiences I accumulated each day contributed to my growth, and that growth expanded my world. There were times when I felt weary from repeating the same process, yet those hours were never wasted. The time that had accumulated had become a force guiding me, and through that force, I found the courage to go further. Each day's time supported me steadily, and within it, my self-belief grew ever stronger.

Part 3 : Self-Management for Goal Achievement

Chapter 1: Setting and Tracking SMART Goals

Setting SMART goals is more than just a simple principle; it has the power to clarify the path to success and bring abstract aspirations into reality. Every beginning is fraught with vague hopes and fears, but establishing a clear plan is enough to keep from losing one's way. The five principles of SMART goals—Specificity, Measurability, Achievability, Relevance, and Time-bound—are the foundational framework guiding daily tasks, as well as the force that strengthens willpower and focus. These five principles help build confidence and a sense of accomplishment over time, allowing me to recalibrate my intentions as I progress.

I first learned the SMART goal-setting method on a construction site. Every aspect of the design and construction process required clearly defined goals each day, along with specific metrics for success. The site was a place that never stopped moving. Time constantly flowed, and I had to focus intensely every day to achieve the assigned goals. This need for goals that were "specific" and "measurable" became evident in the construction site environment. Without clear goals, time would drift away, and any plan lacking detailed steps was prone to collapse.

Once I began to understand this flow of goal-setting, each day's achievement became a small outcome, and these outcomes fueled the possibility of bigger goals. To construct structures within limited timeframes, all goals on the construction site had to be "specific," and at each stage, I needed to check my position and reassess my path. Goals on the site went beyond simply completing tasks; they brought joy—a sense of daily accomplishment as I met each target.

1. Specificity: Visualizing Goals and Finding Fulfillment in Achievement

Every day as I stepped onto the construction site, one principle propelled me forward: "Specific Goals." When a goal was clear and specific, it became not merely a hope or resolution, but a powerful guiding force. Specificity meant drawing boundaries, marking out what I could achieve versus what was out of reach, and understanding where I needed to focus. It was through specificity that I began to realize goals, shaping them with my own hands.

I realized that goals could not remain vague ideas, residing only in the mind. Setting specific goals was akin to unfolding an endless blueprint and following each step. It involved visualizing the goal as if it were already a completed building, then breaking that image down into achievable segments. This approach became my way of pursuing goals, and through this process, I reaffirmed myself daily, finding satisfaction at the end of each day.

How Specific Goals Create Focus and Direction

Specific goals gave structure to each day. Without a clear aim, efforts could scatter easily, but with a defined goal, I could progress purposefully, one step at a time. Specific goals propelled me forward, and as I inched closer to each one, a sense of accomplishment accumulated. The more tangible a day's goal became, the clearer the fulfillment I derived from it.

Each time I established a concrete goal for the day, not only did I know what to do, but also how to accomplish it. Setting specific goals was like reading a blueprint. Just as every wall and column has a designated position, my goal too became a completed plan. Each time I created and acted on specific goals, I reaffirmed my sense of responsibility in the process, strengthening my resolve to achieve.

The Experience of Achievement:
A Journey of Self-Discovery

With each small achievement, I grew more confident in myself. Achievement was not merely a result; it was a way of discovering myself, recognizing my potential. Because the goal was specific, the achievement was more than a number or metric—it was proof that I was moving forward, gradually overcoming my limitations.

The process of setting specific goals and advancing towards them was far from easy. At times, I couldn't complete the goal; unexpected difficulties blocked my way. Yet, because the goals were clearly defined, I was able to stay on course. When the goal was vividly visualized, I could see precisely what I had missed, even in failure. Specificity provided stability and the power to keep moving, even through setbacks.

The True Value of Goals and Achievement in the Field

Each day on the construction site presented a new challenge, which I adopted as my daily goal, crafting small achievements within it. The more specific the goals, the brighter my efforts shone, as I gave my all to accomplish every necessary task. Visualizing a goal was like building a structure layer by layer.

The sense of achievement that grew within me was modest but solid. At the end of each day, I could look back on what I had accomplished and feel a small but clear sense of satisfaction, which fueled my drive toward the next day's goal. Daily goals gradually filled my life with resilience, and the accomplishments I achieved each day made me even stronger.

A New Tomorrow, Powered by the Strength of Specificity

The greatest gift that specific goals gave me was self-trust. When goals are vague or unfocused, commitment can waver easily, but clearly defined goals pointed the way even in uncertain times. When small successes accumulated, forming a foundation under me, I could finally confront myself, honestly and confidently.
Every morning, I revisited the day's specific goals, renewing my commitment to myself. Piece by piece, the accomplishments formed a riverbed of life, a flow carrying me forward. When each day started with a specific goal and ended with its achievement, I could feel with certainty that I was truly walking my own path.

2. Measurability: Building Confidence Through Small Successes

When a goal is clear and measurable, this criterion becomes a powerful tool. With each small success tracked and recorded, a growing sense of certainty emerges, more powerful than any fleeting sense of achievement. At first, I thought achieving small goals was merely part of my daily routine. Yet, as each success accumulated, I found myself growing more confident, seeing the path to my larger goals with greater clarity.

In the beginning, daily record-keeping felt awkward and burdensome. Tracking my progress and reflecting on what I had achieved seemed like self-imposed pressure. However, as I continued to log my progress, I realized that each entry was not merely a number or a line on paper; it was a form of encouragement and a mirror that allowed me to look back and see how far I had come. Each small success brought my seemingly distant goal closer, transforming it from a vague hope into a tangible reality I could almost grasp.

The Power of Recording Small Successes

Sitting down at my desk each night to document my daily accomplishments became a ritual that subtly transformed me. It was just a simple record, but I felt as though each small success was gradually piling up within me, supporting my journey forward. As my log grew, so did my sense of progress. Each night, this process of recording allowed me to reflect, a moment of introspection where I could reassess my direction.

Some days, my records filled me with embarrassment—failures or incomplete attempts dominated the page. Yet even those moments spurred me on, encouraging fresh resolutions for the next day. Together, my successes and shortcomings created a map of my journey, a light showing the road I had traveled. I would pick up my pen again, determined to leave my mark on today, confident that tomorrow's entry would be better. And each time I noticed myself evolving through these entries, a quiet but resolute confidence began to grow within me.

Gaining Confidence Through Small Achievements

No matter the scale of an achievement, recording it daily built up my inner confidence over time. Initially, logging my day felt like a mere chore. Yet as my entries accumulated, I realized I was gradually changing, one day at a time. Yesterday's small success instilled confidence in today, and today's confidence empowered me to hold my future goals with renewed strength. The small successes became a ladder moving me forward, each rung a step closer. Climbing this ladder, I began to believe in myself more deeply.

Through this recording process, I steadily built trust in myself. Each day's success grew my conviction that another was soon to follow. Whenever I felt myself making steady progress, the realization itself was a source of reassurance and strength. Even if the larger success was still out of sight, each small milestone shone like a guiding light along the path, encouraging me to keep moving.

Accumulating Small Wins into Larger Successes

As time went by, I felt my daily achievements finally coalescing into something greater. At first, I questioned whether these minor wins truly mattered. Yet as they accumulated, I began to recognize new possibilities within them. Small wins felt like puzzle pieces that, together, formed a larger picture, and through assembling this picture, I could sense my own transformation. Every day's record became a stepping stone, supporting me on an upward path toward something far bigger.

As I looked back on the path created by my many small steps, I realized the massive journey I had taken. This road wasn't merely about reaching one large objective but was a journey made up of small successes, failures, and lessons, which together crafted a unique and personal path forward. Walking this road, I felt myself growing stronger with each day, each milestone imbuing my life with deeper meaning.

I began to understand that success is not just a matter of achieving a single large goal; it is the cumulative effect of each small step taken along the way. With each day's small success, I grew filled with confidence and conviction, and the further along this road I traveled, the more I believed in myself and the lighter my steps became.

3. Achievability: Understanding and Testing Your Limits

Achievability in SMART goal setting is more than just creating realistic goals. It is about genuinely assessing your limits and potential. Even the most ambitious goal can become a burden if it feels completely out of reach, weighing you down with unrealistic expectations. For this reason, I learned to break down larger goals into manageable steps, gradually accumulating smaller wins. Achievability is a process of self-examination, a way to grow through realistic, reachable goals.

In my role in sales, this principle became a central truth. Every interaction with a client was a test of my ability to explain and persuade. At first, I struggled even to identify realistic goals, as my vision of success was so vague. Yet, with every client encounter, I better gauged the demands and my ability to meet them. Each meeting taught me how to set goals that aligned with my capacities—a lesson reinforced daily through my clients' responses and expectations.

On a particular day, I prepared for a critical contract meeting with a mix of excitement and doubt. I felt the goal was too big and couldn't shake the uncertainty. At that moment, I understood that ambition alone was insufficient. Breaking the meeting down into smaller tasks, I prepared for every question, refining my approach to address the client's needs. Slowly, through carefully executed steps, I gained their trust. These smaller goals became a foundation, transforming an abstract ambition into a concrete, achievable objective.

Realistic Goals Nurturing Personal Confidence

With each small, achievable goal met, I felt an unexpected sense of growth. Goals set within my capacity rewarded me with frequent, fulfilling victories. Each small success led to the next, each growing my self-confidence. The most crucial aspect was not only reaching these goals but also cultivating belief in myself along the way. I realized that by moving forward step by step within my abilities, I could genuinely connect with my path.

In particular, these smaller goals helped me excel during meetings with clients. Every moment I delivered a prepared message with confidence, I did so with the reassurance that I was meeting a goal I could manage. Even in moments of doubt, setting goals within reach gave me a sense of stability. The more these smaller wins added up, the more I trusted myself and gained the stability to confidently handle client interactions. The accumulation of these small successes became an invaluable asset.

Growth Found in Failure

Of course, not every goal unfolded as planned. I encountered failures in unexpected ways, facing disappointment and obstacles. Yet, each setback offered a chance to reassess my goals, leading me to appreciate the importance of smaller successes. Rather than always striving for lofty achievements, I learned to set practical goals within my limitations. Failure taught me not only the value of realistic goals but also how to reflect on myself along the journey.

Goals based on achievability were rarely flashy. Often, they were small and seemingly inconsequential, but the joy they brought was profound. These small wins formed the basis of my growth, helping me nurture self-reflection and resilience. Achievable goals became a testing ground where I could push my potential and stretch my capabilities.

4. Relevance: The Value of Goals That Link Me to My Organization

As I delved deeper into planning tasks, I gradually realized that my goals were not solely for my personal growth but were intricately linked to the organization's direction. When a goal contributes to both my individual development and the organization's progress, it gains a richer meaning. It's no longer just a figure or a product but a "living connection" that binds me and the organization. The passion I felt for my work grew as I worked for something larger than myself, as I sensed that my growth was interwoven with the organization's own evolution.

Initially, I viewed my goals as tools solely for building my career, for achieving personal success. But as time passed, I saw how even small accomplishments could spark broader positive impacts throughout the team and, eventually, the organization. My successes were no longer mere numbers or figures but stepping stones, inspiring my colleagues to set more ambitious goals and build confidence. In an organization, when a person's goal becomes solid and clear, it can act as a 'connection point' that transcends individual effort.

For example, in each project, I found myself gathering the ideas of team members, aligning their diverse thoughts into a cohesive direction, so that small ideas could blossom into major accomplishments. Through this process, I came to understand how my goals aligned with the organization's vision and contributed to both my own growth and the organization's overarching goals. When my objectives were seamlessly woven with those of the organization, they began to carry a significance that transcended individual achievements and became embedded in my daily life.

A Personal Dream and Passion for My Organization's Success

As my goals became more aligned with organizational needs, I found myself filled with an even deeper sense of responsibility. These goals transcended personal success and held the power to contribute to the organization's direction. This value wasn't something that could be measured by a single success or metric. Every effort I made toward these goals became a moment of shared growth for both the organization and myself, a journey that gradually strengthened me. When my aspirations were fused with the organization's vision, I felt that my work became a bridge that truly connected me to the organization.

Take the example of creating a project plan. Each word I chose and each resource I prepared were not simply parts of a task but representations of the organization's direction. This awareness filled me with a sense of pride, even as it raised the stakes. Even a single report felt like an essential piece of a larger puzzle, a fragment that, together with others, painted a grand vision for the organization. When my objectives connected with the organization's goals, the meaning of my work grew richer, and it felt as though I was providing a necessary foundation on the path toward shared success.

The Value of Achievements Realized Together, Not Alone

As I came to understand that my goals were not solely for my benefit but also tied to the success of others, my perspective shifted. My goals now embodied a collaborative journey toward shared growth. Every day I worked toward those goals, they took on deeper meaning. My dedication wasn't just for my own progress but became something that benefited my colleagues as well. When my small achievements positively affected others, my goals evolved from sources of personal satisfaction into contributions to the entire organization.

On the journey toward achieving these goals, I grew increasingly aware of my position within the organization and the broader picture of how I fit into its goals. When goals extend beyond individual success to support organizational growth, I found myself filled with a greater sense of pride. Moreover, the knowledge that my achievements connected with my colleagues' goals brought me a profound sense of satisfaction. With each step toward these goals, I felt an enduring connection with the organization—a realization that my efforts and accomplishments were woven into its future. Each goal achieved gained a meaning beyond a single success.

The Significance of Pursuing Goals with the Organization

Through my planning work, I came to understand that goals gain their deepest significance when they serve as bridges connecting me with the organization. When my success aligned with the organization's growth, my goals took on a depth and resilience they couldn't have had if only serving my own interests. Goals achieved individually can shine momentarily, but those achieved with the organization become foundational and enduring, serving as the bedrock for future growth. These goals were not solely for me or my team; they embodied the collective aspirations of everyone I worked with. My goals became seeds planted for realizing the organization's vision, and as they took root, I found myself growing in tandem.

I grew increasingly certain that the true value of such shared goals would yield greater rewards over time. If my efforts could contribute to the organization's growth, thereby enabling it to reach even higher goals, then I would find genuine fulfillment in my work. This goal, which linked me to the organization, became not just my reason for being there but my daily motivation. My goals were an instrument of growth, a source of pride, and the foundation of my personal development, aligned with the organization's vision.

The goals I set for myself and the organization carried a significance that went beyond my individual accomplishments. Through the organization, I found that my accomplishments pointed to a path I needed to follow, becoming a shared future that I could help shape with my own efforts.

5. Time-Bound: The Power of Keeping Promises to Myself

Every goal carries with it a designated time frame, which is more than just a number—it's a promise I've made to myself. This time limit is a self-imposed discipline, a crucial motivator to help achieve my goals. The boundaries of time demand not only commitment but also the determination to keep pushing forward, especially when I feel the urge to give up. Without a set time frame, goals risk being postponed endlessly, while a time-bound objective intensifies its clarity and urgency.

Time on a construction site exerts an undeniable influence over every goal I set. It's not just a ticking clock; it's the foundation for every structure I aim to complete. Any disruption in this foundation threatens the entire process. In that pressurized environment, each day became a small step on a staircase leading to the project's completion. Just one lax day could shift the goal further away, jeopardizing the entire timeline. A lack of time turns goals hazy, eroding the motivation to strive wholeheartedly.

Strengthened Through the Weight of Time

This pressure, at times, bore down heavily on me. But within that pressure, I learned that time constraints could actually refine and strengthen me, forcing me to be meticulous each day. The presence of deadlines demanded heightened focus, sharpening my resolve. Managing timelines on a construction project, I faced daily reminders that even a minor miscalculation could delay everything. This pushed me to be thorough, to treat even small tasks with importance. The driving force wasn't the goal alone but the dedication to fulfill it within a specific timeframe.

One late night, as I reviewed a delayed project schedule, I realized that the value of time wasn't in the numbers on the timetable. Rather, time was the essence of daily perseverance. Goals with no timeframe can be easily postponed, causing motivation to dwindle. But a time-bound goal carves out a clear path, making each day significant. Within the boundaries of time, each day felt more vivid, giving meaning not only to my work but to my life.

The Weight of Self-Imposed Time

In the construction field, time constraints weren't just external demands but self-imposed commitments that I took seriously. When my goals became personal promises rather than mere tasks, I felt empowered. Though tighter deadlines added weight, that weight made my resolve unshakable. Upholding these deadlines became not just a means to reach my goals but the very reason I pushed forward. I reminded myself that if I failed to honor the set time, all my efforts could dissipate.

When time and goals stood side by side, the goals transformed from mere achievements into personal growth journeys. Each successful day deepened my understanding of time's significance, as the project moved steadily toward completion. Each morning began with renewed determination, and as I wrapped up each day, a sense of progress solidified my resolve.

Discovering Myself Within the Boundaries of Time

A goal without a time limit can fade into oblivion, and the zeal to pursue it may weaken. However, a time-bound goal enriches each day with purpose. As I realized the power of time's boundaries, I felt my drive strengthen, with each time constraint serving as a cherished teacher. The framework of time allowed me to move toward a better version of myself, helping me uncover new paths within myself.

Reaching a goal within a specific timeframe becomes more than a win; it's a promise kept to oneself. The most valuable outcome wasn't just accomplishing the goal—it was proving my own dedication repeatedly. Each morning, I faced time's constraints and embraced them as a guide. By committing to achieve the goal within this time, each day had clarity and purpose, fortifying me further.

Time on a construction site is ever-present, serious, and urgent. To accomplish anything within these confines, I had to accumulate small, consistent efforts every day. And as deadlines approached, the goals acquired a renewed intensity. In these time limits, I was no longer simply striving to complete tasks; I was on a journey to uncover my own character. Within this process of working within time's boundaries, I wasn't just achieving success; I was finding myself.

Accomplishments and Confidence, Built on the Foundations of Time

Setting SMART goals is more than a strategy; it has become the core of my daily achievements, a force that drives my growth. Each day's achievement made my work more meaningful, slowly giving form to the future I envisioned. Goals built upon daily progress accumulated step by step, like ascending a staircase. The small victories brought me closer to my ultimate dream. Those incremental successes became the foundation of my self-belief, pushing me forward. Time became a gift, providing opportunity after opportunity to reach higher, to venture further.

In the passing days, I constantly reviewed my goals, and with each small success, I felt a growing strength within. Setting goals and working toward them was never just a way to complete tasks; it became a means to understand myself more deeply, to explore my potential and limits. As I saw the results of daily accomplishments build up, I gained a profound sense of purpose and confidence. I began to trust that my path was true and that I would reach its end someday.

These accumulated achievements left visible imprints on my life.

They weren't mere markers of completion but foundational pillars, shaping my routine, strengthening my sense of self. Success wasn't a one-time event but an enduring structure that supported me as I moved forward. The SMART framework was more than a planning tool; each accomplishment reinforced my confidence and filled my daily life with pride and certainty.

As time flowed, those small accomplishments grew into substantial achievements, and eventually, my goals were no longer intimidating. They became the guideposts that reminded me where I needed to go. Even in moments of fear and uncertainty, they lit the way, offering direction and purpose.

Setting SMART goals went beyond personal success. It clarified my journey, providing me with the grounding to stay focused. Time continuously shaped and refined my goals, and the accomplishments born from this process became the light illuminating my path.

Chapter 2: Building Confidence Through Small Wins

Discovering the Meaning of Small Successes

When I first set foot in the world of sales, I found myself engulfed in an overwhelming tension. Each time I entered a meeting room, all eyes turned toward me with an intensity that felt both sharp and unfamiliar. In the cold, expectant air, people awaited my words, and in that space, I struggled to find my footing. Time after time, each meeting ended with polite declines and disappointed expressions. "Is this really the path meant for me?" This question, like a seed, began to take root in my mind. Every day felt like an uphill struggle, where even the smallest victory was elusive.

Yet, I couldn't allow myself to give up. I knew I had to start somewhere. So, I redefined my goals—keeping them modest and straightforward. Instead of chasing sales numbers, I focused on simply listening to clients. I committed myself to understanding their true needs and desires, tuning my attention to catch every subtlety in their words. With this approach, I resolved to make each interaction meaningful, to listen deeply, and to make even a single question I asked resonate as genuine interest, capable of drawing out their real thoughts.

The moments spent listening to clients were like walking blindfolded, with only my ears open to hear their unspoken emotions. I heard insecurity and hesitation in their voices, picking up on the undertones of fear or hope. Little by little, I noticed that their voices held clues, subtle but unmistakable. Each fragment of meaning brought a sense of direction, and with each discovery, I felt a quiet confidence blossoming within me.

One day, the first sign of trust came through—a small change in their tone as they responded to my questions. It wasn't monumental, but it was what I had been searching for. The impact of a single small win was more powerful than I'd expected. My disappointment began to recede, replaced by a quiet confidence that each small step was helping me regain my footing. Every minor achievement became a stepping stone, keeping me steady.

These small, modest goals brought me daily moments of joy. They transcended mere performance; they created fragments of trust between the client and me. I felt my own growth with each interaction, my understanding deepening as I learned what clients truly valued. My confidence in myself grew as well. I began to see why I was on this path, piecing together my purpose in the small but profound achievements that punctuated each day.

As these little victories accumulated, I felt myself standing taller. Often, small lessons can be more valuable than big triumphs. Small wins stabilized me, giving me the courage to take on larger challenges.

Finding Seeds of Success in Failure

The road in sales was paved with repeated rejections and closed doors. Each day I knocked, seeking time and opportunity, yet those doors rarely opened. The cold stares, polite but dismissive responses—they were like bruises that added weight to my heart. Sometimes, as I left a meeting room, I felt as though I was walking through a vast darkness. "Is this really the right path for me?" That quiet question lingered, echoing inside me.

But even in those moments that felt like dead-ends, I began to look inward. The rejections were a mirror, reflecting my own actions back at me. I examined myself, scrutinizing my words, my approach, and my intentions. Gradually, unnoticed missteps started revealing themselves.

I realized that certain ways of speaking or posing questions might have come across as pushy, creating distance. Perhaps my eagerness to impress had prevented me from fully understanding the client's perspective. This small epiphany took root within me, and from that point on, I started seeing clients in a new light. I slowed down, listened more deeply, and tried to understand what was unsaid.

Then, slowly, a shift began. Conversations lasted a little longer, clients' expressions softened. Meetings that once ended abruptly now stretched into moments of genuine exchange. This small transformation filled me with a gentle joy. Listening more carefully, truly hearing their concerns, I sensed that I was drawing a little closer to them. Every subtle shift felt like a small success.

Failures continued to visit, but each carried within it a lesson. Each refusal became an opportunity to identify areas for improvement, to reshape myself and try again. Failures were no longer obstacles but rather teachers, guiding me to a version of myself that was a little better than before, a little closer to where I wanted to be.

The rejections no longer felt like closed doors but stepping stones marking my journey. Those small wins anchored me, instilling resilience. From each lesson learned, I grew stronger, and from the seeds of success in each rejection, I felt my roots deepening. I trusted that these hard-earned insights would one day make me more resilient.

Accumulating Confidence Through Small Accomplishments

With each passing day, the accumulation of small wins helped build a sense of inner strength. They weren't grand achievements—just small promises kept, brief conversations with clients, shared laughter, nods of understanding. Each moment was unassuming, yet these little wins stayed with me. What seemed insignificant in isolation grew quietly into confidence within me, like a steady tree taking root. Day by day, this confidence grew deeper, eventually becoming a quiet but unwavering presence within.

There came a moment when a long-pursued client finally chose to work with me. Sitting across from me, he paused before saying softly, "Most people don't listen quite the way you do." In that brief statement, I felt the weight of my efforts reaching him. It was as if every fiber of my sincerity had found its way into his heart. This wasn't simply the satisfaction of closing a deal; it was proof that my intention to understand had come through, that he had sensed my genuine care.

These small wins became the foundation of my self-assurance. Rejections no longer held the same power over me. Even as setbacks continued, I knew they would only make me stronger.

How Small Successes Changed Me

My inner fears began to crumble with each quiet success. Each small promise fulfilled, each client listened to—these moments reshaped me. Nods of acknowledgment, their silent attention to my words, the ways they accepted me on their own terms—all these gestures encouraged me to take another step forward. Each small accomplishment fortified me for the next challenge, providing me with the strength to persist and keep pushing.

Now, rather than setting my sights solely on a grand objective, I understood the importance of small wins along the way. Instead of yearning only for a towering achievement, I was grounding myself in daily successes that allowed me to grow. Each small success was a building block, becoming a steady foundation in my life that empowered me.

Rising Above Failure and the Transformation Brought by Small Wins

Throughout my journey in sales, rejections and failures shadowed me. When a client disregarded my proposal or responded with an unchanging expression, I felt my confidence shrink. Emotions welled up inside me, and each time, my anxiety began to surface. In those moments, I reflected deeply, analyzing what I might have overlooked. Eventually, I realized that these failures were opportunities for growth. They weren't meant to break me but to guide me onto a better path.

One day, facing a crucial meeting, my proposal was met with a cold refusal. My document, my presentation—none of it resonated with the client. My disappointment was immense. Yet strangely, in that moment, I felt a sense of calm. Reflecting on the journey so far, I re-evaluated my attitude and approach. Had I, perhaps, been too focused on my perspective rather than seeing things from the client's? Their silent response conveyed a message: I needed to understand them better.

This realization brought a subtle change. In preparing for my next meeting, I focused not on my own agenda but on the client's needs, carefully refining every aspect of my proposal. I reshaped my presentation to begin from their interests, building it around their concerns. This slight shift, though small, was profound. The clients responded differently, leaning in and showing genuine interest.

In the space created by each minor adjustment, I discovered new possibilities. My understanding of success shifted from one grand vision to a series of achievable, meaningful steps forward. From each small success, I grew stronger, cultivating a resilient confidence that became my foundation.

A New Beginning in Every Rejection

In moments of rejection, I realized I needed to choose my direction forward. Each time I encountered cold reactions and repeated failures, I made a choice not to give up. Through this process, I came to understand that rejection was not failure; it was another step, a necessary one, that strengthened my resolve. Rejections forced me to look inward, to pinpoint overlooked aspects and refine myself. It wasn't the rejection itself that could bring me down—it was my own reluctance to learn from it.

I decided to stop fearing rejection and instead use each instance as a chance to reexamine my approach and attitude. In doing so, small accomplishments began to accumulate, each one building on the last, eventually forming a foundation for larger outcomes. Although rejection sometimes left me disheartened, the insights I gained were invaluable.

Failures weren't walls blocking my path—they were doors to new possibilities. Every time a door closed, I found hidden paths leading elsewhere, glimpsing faint glimmers of possibility within rejection. From each rejection, small seeds of success took root, and I knew they would one day grow into a greater harvest.

Accumulating Achievements, and the Leap of Promotion

As time passed, I moved forward, step by step, one small success at a time. These little, often unnoticed moments, each insignificant on its own, accumulated to form deep imprints within me. My days at the company became an integral part of my identity, a mirror in which I could see myself growing. Then, one day, all the efforts I had poured in were acknowledged—a promotion was offered to me. It was more than a step up the corporate ladder; it was the culmination of every small success, every failure, coming together to open a new door.

That promotion wasn't just a change in title; it was proof that my efforts hadn't been in vain. It was a milestone that reaffirmed my trust in the path I had taken. The confidence I'd built with each small success became my anchor, empowering me to face new challenges without wavering. This promotion was a new beginning, one that came with responsibilities and the chance to grow even further.

The Confidence Born from Successes Stacked Over Time

These small successes weren't won overnight. In the early days of my sales career, I faced indifferent responses from clients and endured countless rejections, yet I persevered. I set achievable goals and made them my compass, focusing on them every single day. I listened to clients, tuned in to their needs, and gradually, bit by bit, inched closer to them. With each small step, I felt a sense of accomplishment, and this accumulation made me stronger, preparing me for even greater challenges.

Looking back now, I can see how these small successes eventually paved the way for a major leap. The trust I built through my work in sales, the knowledge I gained from each client relationship—these became the foundation of a broader perspective. These successes taught me patience and resilience, qualities that helped shape who I am today. Whether facing a setback or a new environment, these small wins gave me the conviction that I could always pick myself up and move forward.

The Moments of Success That Became My Roots

My promotion was certainly an achievement to celebrate, yet it was also the start of a new journey. It meant more than a title change; it gave me a chance to deeply consider my future direction and purpose. This moment reinforced how much those small achievements had grounded me, becoming the roots that now supported my path forward. Each day's efforts, layered one on top of the other, had formed a sturdy foundation that now illuminated my way.

Now, at this new juncture, I see that the journey stretches onward, far into the distance, holding endless opportunities for learning and growth. These moments have instilled a confidence in me, a certainty that I am ready to start afresh, ready to reach beyond what I've accomplished so far.

My small achievements were never merely about proving myself. They became a source of strength that I can draw upon no matter where I am or what challenges I face. They remind me to believe in myself and press forward, always.

Chapter 3 : The Power of Persistence and Motivation

Strength in Steadiness

Persistence is not merely repeating a single step. It is the deep-rooted strength of a tree, standing firm against storms, grounding itself in the soil. This steady resilience was the strength I found as I took on the weighty role of Sales Director. Initially, that responsibility felt overwhelming. The targets given to me were immense, and I felt my steps shrinking under their sheer size. Yet, I came to understand that meeting these monumental goals required more than a singular leap. Each day's earnest effort, every small achievement, was like a stone laid to form a steady path, a path that would allow me to carry the weight without faltering.

Faced with such vast objectives, my steps sometimes seemed too slow, almost inconsequential. Impatience rose within me—wondering how others saw me, questioning if I would truly be able to achieve these goals. My days appeared so small, my actions minor against the enormous expectations before me. Yet, I kept moving forward, even as uncertainty tried to swallow me. I learned, bit by bit, that reaching a goal wasn't about a sudden victory; it was about those daily steps that, though tiny, would eventually bring me to where I wanted to go.

When I looked back over the days and saw them stacking up, my efforts no longer felt meaningless. One day turned into a month, and within that time, I began to find small successes that fueled my steps forward. These small accomplishments became stepping stones, reminders that each daily stride mattered more than a single triumph. Persistence, I came to realize, was not a passive endurance—it was the force that built my trust in myself, a trust that solidified with every day's work.

Persistence, unlike mere endurance, involved the accumulation of meaningful efforts. As these efforts added up, I found within myself a growing resilience, a strength as natural as a tree slowly revealing its branches and roots. Early on as Sales Director, I faced formidable challenges, stumbled through setbacks, and grappled with frustration. There were countless times I wanted to retreat. But each small success along the way became a reason to persevere. The satisfaction of those small victories kept me going even in the face of seemingly insurmountable goals.

To me, persistence became more than just achieving measurable results; it was the process of building trust in myself. Every day felt repetitive and at times unrewarding, but the sense of accomplishment in these small wins grew over time, forming a reservoir of strength. And eventually, one day I realized that these steady steps were not merely adding up to a single achievement. They had created a mountain of confidence, a power that would support me through any challenge. This accumulation of small achievements became my greatest asset, the foundation of my strength.

The goals I set taught me the true value of persistence. Day by day, small step by small step, I began to believe in myself. Each stride transformed me, and at the end of the path, it was not just the achievement waiting for me, but the conviction that I had the resilience to walk any path I chose.

The Anchor of Purpose Amid Shifting Goals

The journey toward my goals was never straightforward. The initial hopes I carried would often lose their sharpness, blunted by reality. At many crossroads, I wasn't sure which way to turn. It was like climbing a mountain—breath grew short, steps became heavy, and I lost sight of the end. But in those uncertain moments, I found my anchor—a quiet strength reminding me why I had started this journey in the first place. This anchor held my purpose and grounded me, recalling the deeper meaning of this path I had chosen.

When I stepped into the role of Chief Construction Officer, I faced an entirely new world. Daily, I encountered complex challenges: the idealism of design clashed with the gritty realities of on-site demands. It was exhausting, and in this struggle, I often felt lost, disconnected from my original vision. I found myself questioning the essence of what I sought to accomplish.

But each time doubt and exhaustion took hold, I grasped onto that original purpose. "When this project is complete, how will people fill this space?" I allowed myself to imagine the footsteps, the conversations, the laughter of future occupants. Though I was entrenched in daily struggles, I knew that at the end of this journey lay a place where people could find comfort, safety, and joy. The thought became a calm strength, a reminder of the purpose within my labor.

Whenever my resolve wavered, I held onto that anchor. It was like an invisible compass guiding me, showing me where I stood and where I needed to go. In times of doubt, it reminded me of the essential reasons why I had chosen this work. Each obstacle reminded me of those who would one day need the spaces I built and the commitment I had made to them.

Holding onto this anchor and moving forward was no easy task. Reaffirming my resolve and taking another step despite fatigue was something I learned to endure, a duty I shouldered as a leader. In the challenges I faced daily—the conflicts, the negotiations—I grew to understand the significance of this anchor. It was the link connecting my past, my present, and the future path I had yet to walk. And with each step, I found myself, not just a goal-seeker, but a stronger version of myself, forged through endurance and resilience.

A Spark That Drives from Within: Self-Motivation

Motivation is like a flickering candle. The smallest gust of wind can dim it, but even the weakest flame holds immense value, illuminating the next step forward. I knew I had to protect this flame. Although it didn't always burn brightly, it was a source of strength when I felt weak, a constant glow that urged me to rise again. There were times I feared its fragility, but I came to realize that it was precisely this delicate flame that had guided me all along.

I once wished my motivation could burn as fiercely as a wildfire, fueling me through every moment. But in time, I learned that true motivation is more akin to a quiet, enduring spark than a roaring fire. It sometimes dims, but it never goes out. The key was to keep reigniting it with small achievements, nourishing it as I continued on my path.

As Chief Construction Officer, the projects before me required immense patience. Results weren't immediate. Progress was gradual, a long series of plans and careful steps. This journey required a deep understanding of why I had chosen it. And within the daily routine, I found that remembering this reason was essential. The small wins made my inner flame burn a bit brighter. Even amid challenging projects, these small moments were the fuel that allowed my motivation to carry me forward.

In the repetitive rhythm of daily work, I sought small joys—not merely to achieve results, but to keep my spirit alive. Whenever a project made progress or a meeting went smoothly, I used these small moments as fuel. These fragments of joy accumulated, helping me understand myself more deeply. Each day's small successes rekindled my motivation. Persistence sustained my flame, keeping it alive even on the hardest days.

In this steady, humble way, I continued on my journey, valuing the soft glow of motivation within me. And that glow, while modest, guided my steps and strengthened me, reminding me that even the smallest flame, when well-tended, can light the way forward.

The Trust and Fulfillment Built Through Persistence

One day, I looked back and realized it was my persistence that had brought me this far. My beginning had been humble. My initial steps were hesitant, slow, and unsure, with a sense of aimlessness about where this road would lead me. Yet, each small step accumulated, creating an unbreakable foundation beneath me. Gradually, my steps gained confidence, and the persistence I had embraced became the unwavering ground upon which I stood, no matter the circumstances.

At first, I thought this journey was mine alone. But over time, my steady efforts began to touch those around me. Colleagues grew to trust my consistency, and my steady presence started to positively shift the atmosphere in the team. I earned a level of respect I'd once only dreamed of, and before long, I was given roles of greater significance within the organization. The small accomplishments I'd accumulated over the years had quietly lifted me to higher positions.

When I was promoted to Head of Sales, I heard something I'd never heard before—someone said I was a leader worth looking up to. The words settled into me like a quiet echo, resonating deeply. As I reflected on those words, I realized they encapsulated all the small achievements and consistent efforts I had made each day. There may not have been grand accolades or spectacular praise, but that single statement became the reason I knew I could continue along this path without hesitation.

Persistence was not simply a method; it became the foundation of trust—both in myself and in others' trust in me. By advancing step-by-step toward my goals, I had gradually built a quiet, unseen faith within those around me. That trust was like an unspoken encouragement. Each day as I rose to work diligently, prepared for another day, my journey became a guidepost for others. My path reached them, and I knew it could light the way for others following behind me.

In the early morning hours, I once wondered if my present self would be unrecognizable to the person I once was, who had started with such small and hesitant steps. As Head of Sales, making decisions and guiding a team daily, I wondered what that younger version of me might have imagined the end of this road would look like. But now I was no longer fixated on the destination. I was simply shaping the road I had been given, knowing that persistence was not a means to an end—it was the path to realizing who I truly was.

When I heard those words of admiration, it felt as though I had returned to the beginning. I remembered the first goals I had set and the tentative steps I had taken. This journey was one in which I had fortified myself, and the small steps I'd taken were finally reaching someone else. My path revealed the reason I needed to keep walking steadily forward.

Persistence became both my method and my goal.

Discovering True Growth at the End of a Long Journey

At the end of this path, I found something greater than the fulfillment of a goal. Reaching the point I thought would be the end, what awaited me was the self-trust and resilience I had developed along the way. Through each day's small efforts and resolutions, I had been steadily, if slowly, growing. The real achievement was not reaching a goal, but in the unshakable belief in myself and the courage to move forward unwaveringly. This courage had become the strength that supported me, turning every step I took into an enduring foundation.

In the beginning, I believed there would be a reward of achievement at the end of this journey. I imagined visible success or measurable accomplishments awaiting me. But with each day that began and ended, what truly remained were not numbers or rankings. It was the invisible marks of achievement: the resolve to take even the smallest steps forward, the promise to myself to keep moving even when I wanted to give up. These repeated moments had become my greatest assets. In the process, I discovered that the path itself, the journey of consistent steps, was the most valuable goal I could find.

There were times when the weight of walking the same path daily felt burdensome. Some days, the monotony of repetition left me breathless. But within this routine, I eventually learned how to walk the road I had been given. Setting goals and advancing step-by-step,

I found that this path had become a familiar part of me. My steps, guided by persistence, gradually chipped away at the towering mountain of my goals.

The true meaning of persistence revealed itself in these quiet moments. In the stillness of everyday life, I grew beyond myself, and the small accomplishments accumulated, gradually propelling me toward larger successes. Achieving something didn't happen in a moment; it was the culmination of countless decisions and steadfastness in action. The trust in myself, the belief in the time I'd spent walking, and the courage that emerged from that journey were the real strengths that allowed me to endure this path.

Sometimes, I felt as though I had lost sight of myself. There were moments when I walked without knowing why or what awaited me, driven only by the promises I'd made to myself. In those times, I would refocus on the idea that my destination wasn't a goal ahead, but a deeper understanding of myself. When I turned my gaze inward, to see myself through my own eyes rather than others', I began to grasp the true meaning of my journey.

There were moments when the end of the road seemed close, only to retreat further, and times when the path felt almost meaningless. But I knew that continuing forward was, in itself, the most precious part of this journey. The countless small steps I'd taken became my fortitude, guarding against weariness. In time, I realized I was not walking this path solely to reach a goal, but to understand myself and strengthen who I was.

The journey I walked became the destination.

This path, which once seemed to end, instead broadened and deepened. Standing on it, I realized there was no need to seek an end. The road wasn't merely a path to a destination. Every step on this path was my destination, and everything I created along the way gave me purpose.

I didn't need to know what lay at the end of the road. Each day's steps had been forging a stronger person within me. The persistence of my steps had introduced me to myself, to someone more resilient than before. Simply knowing that I was moving forward was enough. As I journeyed, I came to know myself more profoundly, each step bringing me closer to who I was becoming. This steady progression prepared me for greater paths ahead.

Even though the road seemed to end, I was still walking it. This path became part of me, and the goal I had once envisioned transformed into a journey of steady, deliberate steps. I had learned that a goal was not about reaching an endpoint, but about shaping myself into a better person along the way.

Now, I no longer felt daunted by the uncertainty ahead. I resolved to keep walking, even if the destination remained unclear. My steps were not just connecting one point to another. Each step was laying a new path for me, allowing me to stand more firmly and move forward with strength.

Walking the road was not merely a means to an end; it became life itself. Along this path, I met myself—my ambitions, my vulnerabilities—and moved forward. As I walked, I came to understand that this journey was shaping me, drawing out the resilience within me.

To this day, I am still walking on this road. The end may be out of sight, but I no longer feel the need to reach it urgently. The path is one that leads inward. And as I walk, I find that becoming a better person, day by day, is enough. This journey was not a destination but a purpose, and each step has become the foundation that supports me.

Part 4: The Art of Communication and Trust

Chapter 1: The Power of Communication – Listening and Feedback

My start in sales came from a single, simple suggestion. The vice president once told me, "There's experience you need to gain among people." This felt like more than mere advice—it sparked a quiet ember inside me. After years of striving toward goals in the field and in design, the word "people" felt somewhat unfamiliar. Goals, efficiency, quality, and results had defined my world. But stepping into sales, I encountered something unexpected: the power of listening, and the trust that arises from authentic communication.

On my first day, I sat across from a client, and everything felt foreign. As I looked into his eyes, I momentarily forgot what to say. Despite all my preparation, my mind went blank as he asked questions, and I stumbled over my responses. Then a simple thought came to me: "Just listen to what he has to say." And so, I began by listening. As he spoke, I slowly came to understand his difficulties and needs—ones I hadn't anticipated. In that moment, I realized that listening was not a passive act; it was a conscious effort to open my mind and genuinely understand another person.

A Conversation Over Coffee

A few months into my sales role, I met with an important client to discuss securing a major construction project. After experiencing several rejections, I felt considerable pressure. That day, the client unexpectedly said, "Shall we have a coffee?" and made the first move to talk. As we walked to the break room, he quietly prepared coffee, and in that silence, I worked to read his intent.

"Let's be honest," he began, holding his coffee cup and looking at me. "I've reviewed your proposals multiple times. But I'm not sure if you truly understand this project yet." His words made me pause. "What matters to me isn't just numbers and plans. I want to know if you understand what this project really means to us and why we should work with you specifically."

That simple coffee chat was unlike any of our previous interactions. It became an opportunity to reflect on myself and how I'd missed grasping the depth of what the project meant to him and his organization. I began to see that beyond the technical details, I needed to connect to the core meaning and impact the project held for them.

After that conversation, I reviewed everything—every piece of data and every approach. I centered my focus on creating value from the client's perspective. That one coffee chat left a lasting impact on my approach to work and my perspective on building relationships.

Learning the Art of Feedback

As time passed, I met many clients, each with their own experiences and needs. Each client wanted something different and brought unique concerns. Through these interactions, I gradually became accustomed to receiving "feedback." Clients were honest, sometimes blunt. If I missed something, they would point it out sharply. If they had questions, they'd ask them directly. At first, such feedback felt intimidating. But over time, I understood that their feedback revealed their genuine needs.

One client told me, "I feel like you're really listening to what I'm saying. I feel comfortable enough to be honest with you." His words touched me. I worked hard not to miss anything he said. The moment I fully embraced his needs as part of my work was the true start of building trust. The more I considered what the client needed to feel at ease, the more I found myself deeply immersed in their story.

Trust is a deep bond that arises when you truly listen to another person.

Trust is that quiet, profound connection born in moments of attentive listening. When we look into each other's eyes and each word settles within us, it creates something indescribable, almost mystical. The best thing I could offer was to listen wholeheartedly to my client's voice. And at that moment, his words began to flow through me as if carving out a new path.

The moments of listening and feedback always awakened something in me. They revealed what I was missing, what I couldn't see. And within those gaps lay hints about the path I needed to take. My clients weren't just contractual partners; they were guides, leading me in new directions and serving as mirrors for self-reflection. In their words were reminders of the things I had ignored, the parts of myself I felt insecure about. Slowly processing those words, I found new clues to the road ahead.

One client gave me particularly tough feedback on my approach. What I thought was fine had fallen short for him. Each word he spoke—courteous but piercing—broke through my defenses and landed deeply within me. As difficult as it was, I listened intently, grasping the essence of what he meant. He left me with a lingering statement: "I'm wondering if I need someone who can see beyond their own perspective." His words left me frozen, showing me where I had faltered, where my vision had not reached.

That night, I replayed his feedback, unable to sleep. Each word echoed within, illuminating the parts of my approach that I had missed. His words quietly ignited a fire in me, pushing me to reflect on everything. The principles I had held tightly weren't necessarily wrong; rather, his feedback allowed them to evolve, to make room for broader perspectives. For the first time, I began to understand how to see the world from my client's vantage point.

After incorporating his feedback, the client showed me deep trust. One day, he said, "Now I feel like you're really the person I need."

In that moment, I grasped the essence of trust. It wasn't something created from perfection; it grew gradually through my efforts to change and improve. Only by acknowledging my shortcomings and working to address them did trust start to reveal itself.

From then on, my outlook widened. I began absorbing my clients' voices more deeply, and as I sought to empathize with them, I held onto their words—even when they felt harsh—as if etching them into my heart. Even when their feedback shook me, I realized it was making me more flexible. In these conversations with clients, I slowly grew.

Over time, I came to understand that clients weren't merely contracts to be won. They helped me uncover directions I needed, ultimately allowing me to understand myself better. They gave me countless opportunities for growth, and our conversations became a journey to renew myself. Trust accumulated gradually; every time I took a step closer to them, they, too, moved closer to me.

I finally understood what communication was. It was a mirror reflecting us both

In the words of my clients, I saw not only their needs but also my own weaknesses. My impatience, my missteps—they were laid bare before them. Humbled, I approached with sincerity and openness. Listening and feedback, two seemingly simple acts, began to take on new meaning within me. Now, I no longer heard their words as mere evaluations; instead, each word became a North Star, guiding my steps. With every stride, my clients watched from behind, casting a silent light of trust.

They opened my eyes, showing me who I was and where I should go. My relationships with clients became like large mirrors, showing me new facets of myself. My inadequacies were gradually refined through their insights. I learned that trust wasn't born from perfection but rather emerged in the moments I exposed my vulnerabilities and worked to fill them. I came to understand that trust wasn't built overnight. It was something we constructed together, step by step, as we opened ourselves to one another's truths.

The true power of communication comes from accepting others as they are

My goals had always been clear: to deliver results, achieve metrics, and advance step by step. But between people, such direct paths faltered. The more I focused on outcomes, the further my clients seemed to drift away, like stones sinking out of reach. The tighter my grip became, the more distant their hearts felt. Again and again, I learned that communication starts not with what I want but with listening to what they want and feel.

One day, I decided to empty my mind and listen fully to a client's story. Simply hearing them wasn't enough. I tried to feel the subtle tremors, expressions, and tension in their hands beyond just the words. My highest aim was simply to hear what they were saying and to sense what they truly desired. Letting go of my own agenda,

I focused entirely on their voice and expression. There were days their stories touched my heart deeply, and other days, they left only a heavy silence.

Gradually, small cracks appeared. No longer skimming over the surface, I began to sink deeper. When I just listened, they opened up. The more time we spent together, the more they began to reveal their inner thoughts. Through listening and feedback, this invisible thread gently tied us closer together. The more I sought to reach the heart of their words, the more they closed the gap between us. The look in their eyes grew more relaxed.

There was one client who often left me feeling uncomfortable, and our conversations usually ended on a cold note. But one day, I decided to listen without interruption, letting him finish. When he paused, I quietly offered feedback: "If I understand correctly, it seems that this part is really important to you." His face softened as he continued. In that moment, I realized that clients open up when they feel genuinely understood.

When I clung only to my desired results, the client relationship would inevitably turn cold. And in those cold connections, I too felt drained. But once I shifted my perspective, focusing on seeing myself through their voices, the story changed. Communication wasn't merely a tool for achieving results; it was a mirror reflecting both them and myself. When I focused on their needs instead of my own, our conversations deepened, and trust slowly took root.

Through these small shifts, I found a new kind of strength. Listening brought me closer to understanding my own feelings and the attitude I brought to my work, while exchanging feedback added dimension to our relationships. The seeds of trust they planted within me began to take root. They began to ask and expect things from me, and I endeavored to honor those expectations and to work with sincerity.

One client once said to me, "It's a relief to know you're genuinely listening." Those words stayed with me for a long time. They taught me that reaching someone's heart requires sincerity. From then on, I resolved to accept each client as they were, regardless of their expressions, and to seek out the emotional threads within their words. The trust that had formed quietly strengthened me from within.

The trust built through listening and feedback wasn't a mere experience. It was a turning point. When we truly listened to each other, the invisible wall between us dissolved. With that wall gone, their words became my story, and my words could finally reflect their true intentions. Communication became a bridge, bringing us closer.

Through my role in sales, I was tested daily. Initially, I struggled under the weight, anxious about results. But over time, I came to understand what true communication was. It wasn't just about listening; it was about accepting the other person as they were, feeling with them, and seeing each other. I looked for what they needed and proposed solutions, and their reactions continually helped me refine myself.

In the end, the power of communication took root quietly within me. I realized it wasn't about goals or performance metrics. It became a compass, guiding me through turbulent moments, lighting the path forward. And only when I finally understood the meaning of true communication did my steps become lighter.

Chapter 2: Building Trust and Managing Relationships

Trust with clients is the cornerstone that determines the start and end of every sales journey. It transcends the mere scope of contracts and isn't something easily constructed or achieved overnight. Trust builds like the quiet passage of time, layer by layer, woven into the texture of deepening relationships. It's not something that can be amassed quickly for short-term results, nor does it come from the difference between yesterday and today. Trust is only earned across long stretches of time—through countless conversations, by honoring small promises, and by committing to understanding each other's core values and needs.

When I first entered the field, clients felt like walls—tall, unyielding. Their gazes, expressions, and even small gestures seemed to speak to the distance between us. Earning their trust wasn't easy. They too were understandably cautious in trusting someone new. Facing their wary looks, I asked myself, What can I give these people? What is it they're hoping to gain from me? To find the answer, I began to open myself up in conversations with them.

This small step became the first move toward establishing trust.

The most important thing in meeting with clients was listening to their voices. I didn't let their words slip by but instead carefully absorbed each one, storing them in my mind. In their voices, sighs, and brief pauses, I tried to uncover hidden meanings. True listening goes beyond just hearing words; it involves empathy—a commitment to understand what they want and what they fear. Clients can sense sincerity. When I truly listened to them, with genuine intent to understand, they slowly began to open up. As clients opened their hearts, our conversations evolved, transcending the simple exchange of information, and moved toward a deeper dialogue rooted in empathy and connection. It was only then that we began to understand each other and gradually build mutual trust.

One client interaction stands out in my memory. He remained guarded for a long time, despite our repeated meetings. I was still untested in his eyes, and he meticulously examined every piece of information I shared, often questioning and scrutinizing each detail. From his perspective, his caution may have been entirely warranted. Through his words and tone, I tried to understand what he hoped for and what he feared. His mistrust wasn't mere suspicion; it was a careful consideration cultivated over years, rooted in his values, attention to detail, and uncompromising standards. To meet his standards, I prepared thoroughly, answered his questions with honesty, and demonstrated my respect for his concerns.

To gain his trust, keeping my promises became paramount. He valued punctuality, tolerating no breaches of time. Showing up on time became a given. Gradually, this reliability allowed him to place a bit of trust in me. Anticipating his needs, preparing materials ahead of time, and making an effort to provide what he might want fostered a subtle shift in our relationship. He came to rely on me for what he needed, precisely when he needed it. Every time I kept a promise, his trust grew, and my commitment to him deepened.

One day, he said, "I think I can trust you with this." That single sentence moved me deeply. It validated all my efforts up to that point while also instilling in me a sense of responsibility to uphold that trust moving forward. In that moment, I realized that trust doesn't come from perfection. It grows when we recognize each other's imperfections and work through them. The trust he extended became a source of strength for me, inspiring me to become a more sincere and dedicated person.

Our relationship extended beyond the bounds of business. It became a partnership in which we recognized and supported each other. After establishing trust with him, I committed to nurturing and growing our relationship even further. Managing a relationship doesn't end when a contract is signed; it is an ongoing process of mutual trust and constant effort toward a better path. Sometimes, disagreements surfaced, but trust gave us the strength to overcome those challenges.

Through this relationship, I learned the profound meaning and value of true communication. In conversations with him, I was no longer just a salesperson. I became someone who listened from his perspective, who sought to understand his needs genuinely. When I presented solutions rooted in his viewpoint, he no longer saw me as just another sales representative but as a partner working alongside him to solve his problems.

In the end, trust is earned through actions, not words. Relationship management extends beyond meeting expectations; it's about surpassing them and delivering something memorable. Every time his gaze softened, every time his voice grew warmer, I felt that our relationship was moving beyond the boundaries of a contract into a realm of genuine trust. Trust grows with time, becoming the solid foundation that anchors a relationship.

The trust and insights I gained through these relationships in sales have provided me with far more than mere success. The trust built with clients has driven my growth, and it remains the source of my purpose on this journey forward.

Trust as a Solid Foundation, Relationship Management as the Structure Built Upon It

Trust was a firm foundation, and relationship management was the structure we built upon it. Building trust took a long time, yet losing it could happen in an instant. With this truth in mind, I approached clients with greater caution, especially those with whom I had gradually built trust through repeated interactions. Trust, formed over each meeting, was not something easily achieved. It demanded my care and complete sincerity.

But beyond building trust, the real challenge was in maintaining it, evolving it into deeper relationships. Trust itself served as a strong base, while relationship management was the daily task of constructing a building upon that foundation. If trust was the pillar bearing the weight, relationship management was like the bricks we carefully placed each day. In managing relationships, I never forced clients to adopt my own goals or pressured them to move too fast. Instead, I took time to understand and respect their perspectives, advancing one step at a time. Trust became the shared construction we built together.

Especially at critical moments of decision-making, I made every effort to provide clients with all the information they might need. I knew it was my responsibility to support them in making choices with full knowledge and confidence. After supplying the necessary details, I allowed clients the space to understand and make thoughtful decisions. The more I respected their decision-making process, the more they trusted my insights. They knew I neither withheld nor exaggerated anything. This transparency made our bond stronger, and I worked tirelessly to honor the trust my clients placed in me.

Relationship management didn't end once a contract was signed; it was, instead, only the beginning. It wasn't just about fulfilling a single promise but about walking alongside clients to strengthen our mutual trust, forging it ever more deeply. As I worked on managing these relationships, I began to feel that our bond had grown beyond mere transactions and into something more profound.

At a certain point, I realized that my relationships with clients weren't simply a means to meet sales goals. They had grown into relationships of genuine respect and understanding between people.

My clients and I respected each other, and they could sense my sincerity in responding to their needs. My clients no longer saw me as a business partner alone. They began to see me as someone who could solve their challenges and deliver the value they truly needed.

This sense of responsibility grew with our deepening relationship. As much as clients trusted me, I worked even harder to uphold that trust. Relationship management became a mutual reliance, a connection we both leaned on. I wanted to be someone who could live up to their expectations. More than that, I wanted to exceed them. Over time, our bond strengthened and deepened as we continued to build upon that trust.

This kind of trust wasn't something that could be measured in figures. It shone through in the small smiles my clients shared, in the natural warmth during our conversations. They began to experience our meetings as more than just business transactions. They saw our time together as moments in which they were truly heard, their needs acknowledged and understood. For me, too, these interactions grew beyond the work itself; they became vital moments of connection and value.

Through this process, I learned how to reach clients authentically. Forcing a point or prioritizing self-interest was never the way to build trust. I was committed to understanding what they truly wanted and needed. The trust we built became more than just a business agreement; it blossomed into a deep sense of connection between us.

With each step I took toward them, my clients opened up a little more. They began to see me as more than just someone who closes deals; they saw a partner who genuinely cared about their needs. The trust they gave me filled me with even greater responsibility. Just as they trusted me, I was determined to honor that trust.

Through relationship management, I came to realize that clients were not just targets to help me achieve my goals. They were the very reason I walked this path, the mirror that reflected my own growth. In giving my best effort to earn and uphold their trust, I grew into a larger version of myself. This process felt like honing and strengthening my own character, becoming a better person.

Ultimately, trust deepened over time, and relationship management was the ongoing process of maintaining and developing that trust. Working together with clients, adapting to their needs while preserving the essence of our bond, I learned that relationships could grow beyond business to become spaces of genuine trust and understanding between people. The trust I gained from clients has become a significant asset in my life, shaping not just my career but also the way I connect with others.

The Value of Trust and Relationship Management Gained Through Experience

As I built relationships with clients, I came to realize that trust is the foundation of every meaningful connection. Trust is not merely a means to close a contract; it's the shared base that allows us to move forward in the same direction, a strong root from which greater value can grow. Trust with clients is not about the success of a single moment, but about the potential to shape a shared future. When trust is firmly established, it opens up new possibilities and mutual growth.

When I first met a client, we were strangers navigating a business relationship, exchanging information and materials to confirm our interests. Yet those first interactions alone could not create a deep bond. Trust isn't built in a day. It forms over time as we listen to each other and as I consistently keep even the smallest promises. By truly listening to clients and working to understand their circumstances, I gradually became someone they could rely on.

Trust is built up slowly over long periods and requires careful management to avoid breaking it. I recall one client relationship that took years to establish. Initially, the client had no expectations of me and seemed only interested in receiving the necessary information, often viewing my proposals with skepticism. I understood that trust would not come instantly.

So, with every meeting, I prepared thoroughly, and I made every effort to keep my promises. As time passed, he seemed to sense my sincerity. Eventually, he began sharing stories about his life and the challenges he faced in running his business. At that moment, I realized he no longer saw me as just a business contact. Listening to his experiences, I began to understand his concerns and thought carefully about how I could genuinely help him.

In conversations like these, I started to see that I wasn't just seeking results but gaining a partner to walk with. As the client shared his story, the trust between us deepened. I learned about his struggles and what he truly needed, which allowed me to provide more meaningful support. Trust was evolving beyond a contract, growing into a relationship built on understanding and empathy.

Through this process, I saw the importance of relationship management. While trust takes time to build, maintaining it requires even more effort and dedication. Fulfilling client expectations, providing the right information when needed, and responding swiftly when issues arise—these are all essential elements of relationship management. Building trust is like stacking small stones, requiring patience and diligence. Along the way, I realized that I was no longer simply a salesperson, but a true partner to my clients.

Trust and relationship management are crucial not only for successful outcomes but also for establishing a mutual foundation. When trust is present, we can respect each other's perspectives and work together toward a better direction. During this process, I noticed how clients' views of me were changing. They no longer saw me as someone selling a product but as a partner invested in the growth of their business.

This trust was possible because I never imposed my goals on them but rather approached each interaction sincerely from their perspective. Relationship management wasn't about simply sharing information or maintaining the contract after it was signed. It was about understanding their perspective, anticipating their needs, and preparing solutions accordingly. Each time a client placed trust in me, I worked to ensure it wouldn't lead to disappointment.

The trust gained through relationship management became a valuable asset for me as well. In the profession of sales, trust and relationship management are not just strategies to achieve business goals. They have become a mirror, encouraging me to reflect on myself and providing motivation to strive for a higher standard. Sales outcomes may be measured in numbers, but the trust and relationships built along the way are true assets I want to hold on to for a lifetime.

Building Trust with the Team: A Confession Over Dinner

"I just couldn't understand why you were always so critical in meetings. It felt like you didn't trust our team."

The words came out cautiously, voiced by a team member at a company dinner, and for a moment, I was at a loss for what to say. The silence we'd left unspoken all this time seemed to surface in that instant, as though it had been waiting for this very moment to break free. The words cut through me, a cool wind stirring inside, yet somehow they felt oddly comforting. I became aware of a distance between us I hadn't realized before, and his honesty made me reflect on myself. What I had intended as guidance to steer us forward may at times have landed as a harsh weight, wounding them in ways I hadn't considered.

"Maybe…" I began, choosing my words carefully, "maybe I was too wrapped up in being right. Sometimes, whenever there were conflicts, I felt an anxiety rise up in me too. I'd worry if I was truly guiding us in the right direction, if this was even the right path for us."

My voice was low and cautious, but within it lay my honesty. For the first time, I laid my own uncertainties and struggles before them. Although my mind wavered, unsure of how they would take it, I hoped somehow my message would reach them. Looking each one in the eye, I wanted them to know I trusted them, though I couldn't predict how my words would be received.

The dinner transformed from a casual gathering into a space where hearts could be laid bare. In the soft clinking of glasses, our long-held silences found voices, each word gently unfurling into the shared space. In the quiet understanding that followed, we began to connect in a way we never had. As my team members revealed their innermost thoughts, I accepted each one, feeling the impact of my impatience, my mistakes, and my intentions more deeply than ever before.

One team member spoke quietly. "Honestly, I just wanted to impress you, but it hasn't always been easy. I wanted to show you that the team was growing, and the harder I tried, the more mistakes I made." This was the first time I'd heard these words, but the depth of feeling behind them was unmistakable. Only then did I see how focused I had been on my own vision, pushing forward without considering how it would impact them. What I had thought of as feedback or guidance had likely felt like a heavy burden to them, weighing far more than I'd realized.

As we shared these moments of understanding and respect, this gathering became something much more profound. It was here, in the gentle stillness of that dinner, that we truly saw each other for the first time. Accepting their concerns one by one, I spoke my truth as well: "I do trust you all. All I ever wanted was to see us grow together." I added this quietly, hoping they could hear my sincerity.

That night, we left with a deeper understanding of one another. They saw the weight of responsibility I carried, and I began to understand the pressure they felt. The dinner was no longer just a conversation—it was a small bridge we'd built together on our path forward. As each of their words touched my heart, I could feel the burdens we'd each been carrying gently lift.

Our shared truth spread gently across the table that night.

For me, trust and relationship management had never been merely tools to achieve sales or professional success. Rather, they were the way I connected with people and grew along with them. Relationships with clients, connections with my team—these were like cherished bonds in my life, precious links that taught me how to grow alongside others. The time and care it took to earn trust left behind a legacy of value that extended far beyond any business goal; it held meaning for my clients, my team, and me.

Chapter 3: Persuasive Communication Skills: Moving Minds and Inspiring Trust

The process mattered, but a true professional was measured by results. The day I proposed the hotel project for the vacant Expo site in Yeosu, I was not merely presenting a plan. I was making a promise to deliver results and, before the stakeholders, my words had to transcend mere explanation—they needed to sway minds. This wasn't a matter of pitching passion and vision alone; it was about shouldering the responsibility to see it through to the end. This project represented more than a simple proposal—it was my chance to prove that I could turn an ambitious vision into a reality.

Beginning with Vision and Persuasion: Designing Possibility

When I first introduced the project, the reactions were measured and, beneath polite nods, I sensed cautious doubt. Building a hotel on Yeosu's Expo site was a bold concept, and the risks were not insignificant. Memories of past projects that had stalled or ended unsuccessfully loomed in their minds, along with thoughts of the substantial capital such an endeavor would require. I needed to design a future compelling enough to shift those ingrained reservations.

To convey the full value of this project, I pored over data and refined projections night after night, sketching out a blueprint for the future I envisioned. I illustrated the tourism potential of the hotel, the anticipated influx of visitors, the economic boost to the area, and the creation of a vibrant new space where people could make memories. I didn't just bring numbers; I presented a vivid picture of a thriving destination they could practically see before them.

But for this to succeed, I had to make the project more than a daring experiment or a risky proposal. I needed to clarify the "possibility of success" that lay within it. While I meticulously organized the figures, projected returns, and economic impact, I knew that data alone would never be enough. Numbers and facts were simply tools—the real aim was to reveal my conviction and the future I envisioned. Through my words and visuals, I sought to help them experience that future, clearly and tangibly, so they could believe in it as much as I did.

I wanted them to understand that this was not just a promising opportunity, but a feasible, actionable plan with genuine potential for success. Backed by success stories and examples of regional economic uplift, I shared case studies to emphasize the unique promise of the Yeosu Expo site. Through repeated simulations and refined presentations, I anchored my vision in facts while revealing the potential I saw in every facet of the project.

In this meticulous effort, I began to kindle a spark of confidence within them. The simulations, the comprehensive data, and my unwavering commitment gradually started to shift their outlook. Bit by bit, I sensed their initial skepticism transform into curious engagement. In that shift, I recognized that persuasion isn't just about conveying words; it's about instilling in others a spark of the possibilities you carry within.

Earning the Owner's Trust: The Power of Authentic Persuasion

But the real challenge came with the final stakeholder: the owner. He was a seasoned veteran who could dissect the vulnerabilities of any proposal with an unerring eye. To persuade someone like him, I knew that simply offering a logical and polished presentation wouldn't suffice. True persuasive communication demands sincerity—an authenticity that assures the other person that they can trust in the vision.

When I met with the owner, I focused on demonstrating realistic goals, achievable budgets, and reliable outcomes. Yet I was transparent about the challenges too, detailing the potential risks and the dedication needed to overcome them. Persuasion wasn't a one-sided argument; I encouraged his feedback, candidly admitting areas I could improve, and allowing him to see the depths of my own commitment to this venture. What he valued was not just a promising result but the assurance that I was genuinely invested and prepared to navigate the entire journey.

In the end, he nodded in quiet approval, signaling his trust in me.

Proving through Results: The Persuasion of Action, Not Words

What remained was to prove it through results. As Head of Planning, my role in this project was clear: rather than being physically present on-site, I was to orchestrate everything from headquarters, ensuring each phase proceeded seamlessly. From design and scheduling to material supply and budget allocation, each step demanded flawless execution with no room for error. My attention to detail had to be absolute.

Managing this project from headquarters was far more than drafting plans. I had to constantly monitor the progress, ensuring each milestone was met according to schedule, while preparing immediate solutions for any issues that arose. This required continuous coordination across departments to marshal the necessary resources and carefully adjust costs within budget to maximize impact. Unexpected challenges inevitably cropped up, prompting me to recheck team schedules, update documentation, and quickly devise contingency plans to keep us on track.

My role was to balance budget and schedule to drive the best possible outcome, while harmonizing contributions from various departments. This coordination was demanding—ensuring each team's role aligned into a cohesive workflow required patience and precision. My responsibility was to streamline these operations so that every department could fulfill its part effectively, enabling the entire project to progress smoothly.

At each stage, I closely monitored progress, proactively identifying potential issues before they could disrupt the flow. When challenges did arise, I addressed them decisively, devising solutions and incorporating feedback from all angles. My knowledge of each detail in my purview allowed me to react swiftly and keep the project on its intended course, preserving the timeline and goals we had committed to.

Finally, as construction wrapped up, we met both our budget and schedule targets. The client's response exceeded expectations, and I felt the full weight of our efforts pay off. Thanks to rigorous management from headquarters, the site team encountered few disruptions, allowing the project to be executed efficiently and establish a foundation of trust.

Through this project, I learned that genuine persuasion isn't about making promises—it's about showing accountability and delivering tangible results. The outcomes of our months of meticulous planning and management spoke on my behalf, proving that action is the most powerful testament of intent. And it was through this action that I offered the strongest proof of my commitment and capability in this role.

Part 5: The Power of Challenge and Overcoming Crisis

Chapter 1: The Mindset of Turning Crisis into Opportunity

Learning to Support Myself Amidst Crisis

In 2008, when the Lehman Brothers collapse shook the global economy, my project was shaken as well. Although the crisis initially felt like a distant event, it soon came to my doorstep. The barren plains of Mongolia were cloaked in cold winds, and there, in the vast and empty expanse, my project stood still, feeling even more desolate than the landscape. In that moment, the crisis was no longer someone else's story—it was mine.

Standing alone in that gusting wind, I asked myself, What can I do now? and What must I hold on to? Then, I realized something profound—the answer lay within me, along the path I had traveled. While the world around me seemed to stop, I knew I couldn't afford to. I had no choice but to trust myself and move forward.

Unyielding Perseverance in the Face of Crisis: A Bitter Mongolian Winter Night

That night, the stars filled the sky, dazzling as if they might spill over. Mongolia's winter nights are pitch dark, yet the stars shone like scattered diamonds in the silence. I stood for a long time, gazing at that distant light, enveloped in a silence so deep that it felt as if the stars were watching over me, whispering words only I could hear. I felt as though they were saying, Thank you for coming this far. And so, I stood there, feeling a quiet sense of solace.

Days passed, and each day was a battle against Mongolia's unforgiving winter. Construction deadlines slipped away, and the bitter cold kept sleep at bay for everyone. My team's faces grew wearier, and the site itself seemed to fall silent, holding its breath. Yet, I could not give up. Every day, I carried the weight of the time and effort we had poured into this project. The frigid air itself seemed to tell me that I couldn't abandon what we had started.

As I turned to head back to my quarters, the sky once again gripped me, blanketed in stars. It was a sight unlike any I had seen. The stars stood still, glimmering with unspoken patience. Even the wind held its breath as the quiet night enveloped me. Looking up at the stars, I sensed the path I had taken and the one that lay ahead. Moments of failure and resilience, sleepless nights, and the countless times I had pushed forward—these memories were etched within me like the constellations above.

In that instant, I knew: the place where I now stood was the path given to me. The colder the night and the longer the journey, the more meaningful each step would be. Though the urge to turn back welled within me, those stars seemed to show me that the road forward lay right here.

Under that starlit sky, I buried my hands in my pockets, feeling my resolve strengthen with each step. Amid the vast expanse and frigid night winds, I met myself on a deeper level. The challenges that faced me weren't just obstacles; they were also my trials, shaping me, forcing me to grow. The bitter Mongolian winter might have rattled me, but the stars remained, steady and silent, as if to remind me to stand strong. And with the stars as my silent witness, I made a promise—to guard my spirit as steadfastly as the stars held their place in the night.

Forging a New Path When the Road Ends

The dream that birthed this project was not a simple one. I had envisioned a barren land gradually filling with people, a new residential complex infusing it with vitality. But as reality set in, that vision began to slip further away. Investors withdrew one by one, and those who remained gazed at me with weary, uncertain eyes. They had once followed me with trust, but now that trust was being eroded by the creeping shadows of doubt. From their looks, I understood: it wasn't just my own resolve I had to safeguard—I was responsible for their faith and expectations as well.

When there was no visible path forward, the only option was to carve out a new one. Every morning, I set out on solitary walks, inhaling Mongolia's biting dawn air. As I gazed across the vast, desolate expanse, I began to discern a trace of potential hidden within it. Despite its barrenness and cold, this land held a quiet, resilient promise. No matter how much the world shook, the ground beneath my feet remained steady. Somewhere in that soil lay a glimmer of hope.

With that possibility as my anchor, I rewrote proposals, recalibrated revenue projections, and reevaluated feasibility. None of it was easy—it was as if I were designing a road from scratch, trying to hold onto every element of my initial dream. Perhaps it was a reckless endeavor, but that reckless resolve was all I had left. And I threw myself into it with everything I had.

Rebuilding Trust Through Solitude and Struggle

At times, I felt I wasn't truly alone; yet, in truth, I had only myself to rely on. The team was exhausted, the investors had receded, and people were beginning to question my every decision. Amid the isolation, I returned to the conviction that had ignited this project. My lone remaining asset was my belief—that even if the journey was slow and arduous, this project could bring renewed hope to those who needed it.

No matter how much I explained or illustrated potential outcomes, there was a persistent doubt rooted deep in their minds. Words of persuasion were no longer enough; I needed tangible proof. I had to demonstrate that I was capable of making things happen.

But how could I achieve that? Inside, doubts swirled like gusts of wind. Had I chosen the wrong path? Was it wiser to stop right here? In moments like these, I found myself searching my own depths for resilience. Even as the world seemed to quake, I reminded myself that I had to forge ahead—that there was no other road for me but this one.

And so, each day, I found ways to steady myself. I wrestled with sleepless nights, pensive walks, and endless reflection. I knew I had to produce results, and I poured every ounce of my strength into achieving them.

In Moments When Nothing Is Certain

I had no way of knowing when success or failure might come, nor could I foresee its form. Whether this path was the right one felt shrouded in doubt, and at times, everything seemed to sway in and out of focus. But there was one thing I knew for certain: this was the path I had chosen. At the end of countless crossroads, I had walked onto this road, and now there was no one else I could hold responsible. When crises loomed and unforeseen moments shook me, I looked back and realized that only one option remained: to see this path through to the end.

Though the way felt heavy and progress slow, I resisted the urge to push myself too hard. Instead, I moved forward, step by step, engraving each decision with quiet resolve. The more everything I once knew blurred, and the anticipated way forward faded into ambiguity, the more I began to question myself. Why had I chosen this path, and what was I seeking? In that process, I finally began to hear my truest inner voice—a voice born not from external tremors but from the steady resonance of my own conviction. That conviction became a solid force within me, one that stood unyielding before fear, a determination strong enough to transform crisis into opportunity.

In those moments of absolute uncertainty, I reached a deeper understanding. Conviction, I discovered, is the single belief that can sustain me when reality seems to crumble; it is the small but unwavering light that guides me when the path grows dark. No matter how the world shakes around me or how the outcomes push me away, each time I found the strength to hold onto myself, that conviction became stronger. As I walked on, despite the conflict and anxiety along the way, I came to see myself more clearly through the haze of uncertainty.

What I clung to was my own conviction. It was that conviction that empowered me, and as long as I held it close, I would not fall—even if everything else seemed to waver. Though the road ahead sometimes felt daunting and uncertain, within my resolve to keep going, I found, at last, my truest self.

The Small Light Sparked by Self-Belief

The success I once envisioned was no longer about reaching a distant goal. It wasn't a towering achievement or external accolade, but a journey that allowed me, day by day, to affirm who I was and to quietly prove myself through each step forward. In those early days, I saw success only as the act of reaching a goal, and each obstacle seemed overwhelming and immense. But as I crossed countless thresholds, I began to see success in a different light. True success, I realized, was not simply about reaching a goal; it was about walking a path that allowed me to affirm my beliefs, steady my resolve, and meet an unshaken version of myself.

In moments when the road seemed to end, in times when I felt cornered by what seemed like dead ends, I found the courage to carve new paths. To others, those times might have looked like failure. Yet I moved forward, one step at a time, and discovered that my aspiration was not just about crossing a finish line. Each step was a process of solidifying my conviction and fortifying my dream. With each hardship and challenge, I came face-to-face with my true self. What I truly sought wasn't simply reaching an end but rather preserving my inner voice and convictions, unshaken.

The strength to believe in myself wasn't monumental. It was a quiet voice within—a small light, flickering in the darkness—that continued to burn even when I felt overwhelmed. At times, my heart whispered, urging me to give up, to let go. Yet, even as I faced these doubts, I learned to believe in myself. That small light, though modest, fueled me. It kept me standing through the darkest of times, a tiny ember of trust that never went out. Even when I felt lost, that ember illuminated my path, guiding me forward and grounding me with a quiet but persistent strength.

The lessons I gained through facing crisis have become my most invaluable asset, more precious than anything the world could offer.

These were not merely experiences but indelible marks that fostered my growth, deepened my inner strength, and fortified my spirit. And within these marks, I was finally able to meet my truest self. When all the trials had passed, what remained was not the judgment of others or the world's fleeting attention, but the quiet trust I held in myself and a small, steady light that testified to the journey I had traveled.

Chapter 2: The Attitude Toward Failure

Out on the plains of Mongolia, the project stalled, frozen like the land beneath it. Every piece I had built, every spark of vision, seemed to slowly fade, leaving no trace of the flame it once held. I found myself in the heart of that failure, where all my plans seemed to dissipate, blown apart by unforeseen winds. The air felt cold and desolate, and everything I had depended on to sustain me began to waver. Failure, as I came to realize, was an unyielding reality. The once-clear goals grew hazy, and there were countless moments when I questioned what had drawn me down this path in the first place. Failure loomed as though it might swallow me whole, filling me with doubt about my place on this journey.

The Weight of Failure in the Bitter Air

Mongolian winters are harsh and unyielding, cutting through to the bone. The frigid wind tore at my plans, shaking the solid foundations I had so believed in until they flickered and eventually faded like candlelight in a storm. The moments of failure came quietly, one by one. First a misstep, then another, each mistake trailing another until they crept into me like an inevitable tide. In hindsight, they seemed to test me as though each were a breath of wind both testing and breaking me.

During those moments, I took in the wounds that failure inflicted on me. In the quiet, when there was nothing I could do to reverse it, questions I had buried began to surface. What was it that I truly sought at the end of this road? I saw, with a painful clarity, that what I desired most was the strength to rise again without losing myself, a strength I had not known I needed.

A Small Belief Found Among Fractured Hopes

And yet, amid the darkness, a faint light appeared. A deep and steady wish to build something on that cold, barren land still flickered within me, despite all that had gone astray. In the heart of failure, I was not grasping for a grand vision or a towering success. What I sought was simply a reason to keep standing, a quiet belief that I could start again. This belief did not suddenly arrive to steady me; rather, it had been taking root slowly, cultivated by the repeated falls and quiet moments of self-confrontation over time.

What I saw in the depths of failure wasn't anything monumental. It was simply the quiet persistence that helped me rise each day. It was like a seedling, sprouting in the soil of a heart that had been broken. Standing out on that vast, unforgiving plain, I allowed the things slipping from my grasp to fall. I began walking anew, step by careful step, planting small seeds of possibility in the barren spaces failure had left behind. Although my plans had crumbled, I found the strength to start filling that emptiness again with what small actions I could take.

Rediscovering the Path, Moving Slowly but Steadily Forward

One day, in the midst of a daunting fog where I felt lost, I finally found my direction. Just when I thought all paths had closed, the very absence of a road began pointing me toward a new way. What failure had taught me was not simply the sting of defeat but the resilience to find a new step even in despair. Amid the fierce winds of Mongolia, I embraced my failures and stood once more. Failure had brought me down, yet it had also left within me a quiet strength to walk forward again.

The power to forge new paths was the deepest mark that failure left behind. Though it had the force to break me, failure also became the very thing that strengthened my foundation. In time, I understood that this was all a part of my growth. Failure was not a sealed door; it was a threshold, an opening to continue forward with new resolve.

Confidence Born from Repeated Failures: The Glass Wall in the Office

In the center of the office stood a tall glass wall stretching from ceiling to floor, looming heavily in my mind. Each time I walked past it, a faint tremor arose within me. That glass wall bore silent witness to countless meetings, countless projects, and among them, the lingering traces of unfinished or failed endeavors glimmered painfully. Standing before that wall, I confronted everything I had missed, every oversight and misstep, the small judgments and miscalculations. The word "failure" seemed almost etched into the transparency of that glass.

Not long ago, a project I had poured myself into came to nothing. Every report and proposal I had carefully prepared was met with cold glances and blunt feedback. As I left the meeting room, the papers I held felt unusually heavy, as though laden with my own helplessness and regret. Passing by that glass wall with a somber expression, I caught sight of my own reflection, appearing so small in its transparency, as though it reflected back the weight of all my burdens.

Yet, over time, I came to see the wall differently. It was not just an unforgiving surface; it was also a mirror, quietly reflecting both the road I had walked and the path I needed to begin again. As I passed that wall, there was a growing sense of both fear and exhilaration, as I began to realize it represented an arena of continuous growth. The moments of failure, rather than bringing me to my knees, were laying the groundwork for the strength to rise.

One day, passing that glass wall, I paused. If I hadn't seen my own failures reflected in it, I thought, perhaps I would not have feared that wall. But now I knew what lay beyond it—my own growth, bound up in every challenge. That glass wall had become a reflection not of defeat but of the invisible road of resilience I was learning to walk. Each time I saw my reflection in it, I understood that the power to keep walking was woven into the promise to rise again, even under the weight of past failures.

At the next meeting, as I walked past the glass wall, I quietly whispered to myself, "Even if I fail again, I will not turn back from here." My reflection in the glass was no longer small. Despite the scars of past failures, I saw someone ready to walk forward, someone whose resolve had been shaped by every setback, no matter how quiet or daunting.

"Just One More Day, Please"

There was a moment when everything almost fell apart, right on the brink of closing a critical contract with a major client. While handling an overseas project, an unforeseen problem arose, putting the entire deal in jeopardy. With the company's fate hinging on this agreement, we had to make a decision by the next day at the latest.

After much deliberation, I made one final request to the client's representative. "Could you wait just one more day?" I knew I was asking for a lot, but I couldn't help but appeal earnestly. He paused for a moment and then nodded.

That night, I gathered all relevant departments, and together we explored every conceivable solution. The night was intense, yet by morning, we had crafted a final resolution. I presented it to the client representative, and thankfully, he accepted it. We saved the contract, barely but surely.

This experience taught me the power of persistence, the strength that even a single day of unwavering effort can bring. I learned the true essence of leadership and how, in the face of crisis, a single extra day can change everything.

A Cold Night and the Urgency of Resolve

One winter, the company faced a dire financial situation. Delays in projects, market shifts, and stalled investments had left us uncertain about the future. As a leader, I felt helpless and weighed down by guilt, as though I'd let down my colleagues and team members.

One midnight, I found myself standing on the rooftop, looking out over the distant city lights. The cold wind pierced through me, but with it came an overwhelming sense of resolve. I promised myself that if given another chance, I would stake everything on it.

As I climbed down, I realized that instead of fearing failure, I needed to seek renewal even in its depths. From that night onward, I tackled each issue step-by-step, gradually rebuilding confidence and finding new investors willing to take a chance on us. That cold night's resolve became my guiding light, strengthening me in the face of any challenge.

Finding Strength at the Edge, Not Looking at the End

When I first faced failure, it felt like the end of everything. The weight of it pressed down on me, as though I were standing before an insurmountable wall. But as I stopped in front of that wall, I gradually realized that it wasn't an end but another doorway.

Standing on the edge of failure, I began to see unseen paths and found within me a renewed strength to rise.

In the depths of despair, I encountered a new version of myself. Failure didn't just take something away; it posed profound questions. "Why did you choose this path?" "What purpose do you serve in this moment?" "How will you respond to this setback?" These questions echoed within, and through them, I uncovered my deepest convictions. I realized that every failure had come not to bring me down but to make me stronger.

Over time, failure became less of an adversary. Although it left painful scars, those marks made me resilient, becoming the bones and flesh of my growth. Failure wasn't a reason to stop; it was an opportunity to learn and start anew. At the end of each failed attempt, I found the resolve to rebuild myself, constantly realigning with my purpose. In each moment of downfall, I rose again, guided by the quiet lessons failure imparted.

Failure also gave me the gift of self-reflection. As I pursued new challenges and faced inevitable failures, I discovered my true self hiding beneath layers of expectation. The journey that began with admitting my weaknesses soon became a path filled with potential for growth. Failure refined me, shaping me into a person of greater value.

Once I understood that failure wasn't the end, I grew curious about what lay beyond. Each setback became a doorway that led to new possibilities. With each door I opened, I grew stronger, gaining a broader perspective. And on this path, paved by the lessons of failure, I continued to push my own limits, discovering new opportunities at every step.

Rather than being crushed by an impending end, I found the strength to move forward from it. The resilience failure gifted me was more than just the ability to stand again; it became a pillar that allowed me to live with unwavering determination. Today, that pillar within me continues to drive me forward.

Chapter 3: Succeeding with Tenacity and Patience

Every time I stepped through the company doors, I steadied myself. I never knew whether the day ahead would bring new challenges or pass quietly. My career in sales had been tough from the outset, demanding resilience day by day. To stand here today, I'd had to climb countless steps, one by one. Each request, every rejection from clients taught me how to persist without losing my way and how to hold my head up and move forward. Through these steps, my patience and tenacity grew, solidified each day.

The journey was never easy; every step along the way was uphill. But the lessons and growth gained from that path were invaluable. Through every promotion, through each new responsibility in planning and management, I learned that it was perseverance that had brought me here.

At First, Everything Felt Overwhelming

When I first stepped into the sales field, it felt like standing alone as a solitary tree in the midst of a fierce wind. Every day was filled with rejections and failures, which, like relentless storms, forced me to dig my roots deeper and find strength in enduring. The demands of each client felt like a turbulent force, and closing even a single contract required me to confront countless setbacks and challenges. The weight of growing responsibilities seemed to overwhelm my every move, and taking even a single step forward became a struggle. But I couldn't give up. Resilience isn't something innate; rather, it's forged each time we surpass a moment where giving up feels tempting. Little by little, every moment of determination layered within me, eventually building up the strength that now holds me firm.

A New Challenge: Transitioning to Strategic Planning

The trust I had built in sales opened up a new opportunity for me: a role in strategic planning. Stepping into that role felt like entering a world entirely different from sales. Planning demanded a new lens, a fresh perspective on everything I thought I understood. In sales, moving a client's heart was key; in planning, every moment was governed by data, strategy, and meticulous calculations. It wasn't the familiar path I knew, and every day felt uncertain. Projects wavered in the face of countless variables, and each mistake felt like a blow to my confidence. Month after month, tangible results seemed distant, and each setback felt like another test of my resilience. Yet, even then, I found a way to steady myself. With every approaching failure, a deeply rooted will surfaced within, giving me the strength to persist through each challenge.

Each time a project failed, I questioned myself: What had I missed? What needed improvement? The questions seemed endless. I'd stay late after meetings, revising plans until the early hours, refining data and reports until sunrise. Pouring over numbers, rewriting objectives, I taught myself to confront and overcome my fears. In the maze of targets and figures, I often felt lost, but I learned to lift myself up again. That journey, though painful, infused me with a strength that kept growing.

Looking back now, I realize that time made me resilient. Those countless days and the cycle of setbacks and doubts had, over time, hardened my resolve. Eventually, facing the daily grind and rallying my spirit became second nature. My preparation wasn't just for reaching goals; it became an ongoing practice of refining and safeguarding myself. Every small decision, made and followed through each day, strengthened me. These layers of resolve became the force that propelled me forward.

The hours and efforts I invested became the bedrock upon which I stand today. Through small failures, my patience and perseverance have accumulated. I know now that this journey isn't about reaching a single peak. True success, I've come to understand, lies in this continuous process of strengthening oneself, of choosing to move forward each day despite the hardships.

Perseverance Wasn't Just Enduring Pain

Perseverance wasn't just the capacity to bear pain. As I navigated the contrasting worlds of planning and sales, I realized that perseverance meant more than enduring suffering. It was about finding a way forward even in the pitch darkness, searching for any slivers of hope amidst despair. Moving through tunnels with no clear end in sight, what mattered most was that I never stopped taking steps. Even if today's steps seemed small and unremarkable, they were the foundation upon which tomorrow's journey would build.

Some days, even the morning commute to the office felt distant and foreign. The weight of the day's responsibilities pressed down on me, leaving me barely able to breathe. As I filled draft after draft of proposals with countless numbers and words, each attempt felt misaligned, as though nothing truly connected. There were days when learning from failures seemed overwhelmingly elusive. Yet, one day, I began to realize that small accomplishments were steadily accumulating. These were not grand successes, but they held me up—each one like a grain of sand building a vast sandcastle. Day by day, each step slowly filled the shape of my journey.

At the end of exhausting days, I would sometimes ask myself, Is this truly the right path? The question stirred my doubts and fears, forcing me to confront my faltering self. But even on those difficult days, there was one thing I never let go of—a faint spark of determination clinging to my fingertips. That faint glow at my fingertips guided me through the dark, a subtle yet steady reminder of my purpose.

I gradually realized that perseverance meant far more than simply withstanding hardship. It was about continuing to seek a path forward, to grasp new possibilities as circumstances continually shifted. It meant not being overwhelmed by the weight of each task but instead holding fast to all available choices, exploring every avenue to its fullest. Those countless nights spent drafting proposals, those hours refining data and recalculating figures—each of these moments anchored me in a sense of profound responsibility, and that weight only served to fortify me further.

No matter how tough the days were, the one thing I had to hold on to was the steady rhythm of my steps. Each one was deliberate, even if slow, and in those careful steps, I found a source of resilience. My stride grew surer, slowly soothing the fatigue within me, and gently guiding me along the path I was meant to take. Perseverance became the courage to trust in myself and move forward, rooted in the belief that today's efforts would shape the person I would become tomorrow.

Now, I understand that true perseverance lies in pushing forward despite all fears and uncertainties, in refusing to lose sight of myself along the way. It's knowing that every step forward, even through the shadows, is an act of quiet courage that leads me, unwaveringly, toward the next horizon.

The Continuity of Projects and the Meaning of Patience

The nature of planning work meant that one challenge always awaited after another. Just as one project neared completion, another was already lined up, eager for my full attention, leaving no moment for respite. There was no time to become familiar with a rhythm; each project arrived with unique issues, testing my resolve in new ways. Every time a new task appeared, I had to brace myself and pour my all into it. This relentless demand was the fate of a planner, a fate I'd come to accept with every fiber of my being. Sometimes, the weight of responsibility pressed down so heavily it felt stifling, yet this weight was also what anchored me here. Patience, for me, was no longer a choice but a necessity—a pillar holding me steady on this path.

One project, in particular, threw a series of unexpected challenges my way. The initial budget began to spiral out of control, and the circumstances drifted far from our projections. Customer demands grew, and within those evolving expectations, my responsibilities felt increasingly burdensome. The project felt like a ship adrift in the vast ocean, and I was left wrestling with unease and confusion. I struggled to regain my footing, doing my best to recalibrate every day amidst ever-changing conditions. But this was not an easy journey. Every night, I'd question myself, wondering if I was truly on the right path and if I could shoulder the responsibilities I had taken on.

Yet, what kept me grounded was a patience that refused to falter, even when success seemed remote and my chosen path unclear. The only thing I could rely on during this journey was my tenacity. In the daily turbulence, I reminded myself that success wasn't a grand, singular achievement. Rather, it was a tapestry of small, steadfast steps—incremental progress built upon layers of resilience and quiet persistence.

Through this challenging experience, I came to understand the deeper significance of patience and accepted its weight. Patience wasn't simply about resisting the urge to give up; it was about holding onto myself in moments of despair and finding the strength to rise again when lost. Even when I feared I might never reach my goal, I focused on the small tasks within my control. The commitment to advance, even slightly, each day, wove the fabric of my path, leading me toward steady growth.

Even though the journey felt endless, I learned that each step was part of a process making me stronger. On that path, I cultivated resilience, celebrating small victories and holding onto patience as a lifeline to withstand setbacks. Eventually, the project passed from my hands into those of the client, and I could take a small sigh of relief as I prepared for the next challenge.

The end of each project always marked the beginning of another, yet the patience and endurance built during each endeavor became my foundation. Patience was no longer merely a tool; it was my constant companion as I forged my path forward.

The Fulfillment That Comes From Small Successes

As every small success accumulated, I felt my confidence solidifying bit by bit. With each step toward a project's milestones, I experienced brief moments of relief and joy. Yet sometimes, the results fell short of expectations. Even then, I didn't allow myself to stop. On days marked by failure, I lifted my head with the resolve to learn at least one lesson and took another step forward. These daily efforts coalesced over time, eventually forming a foundation strong enough to support me. I came to realize that perseverance wasn't just about moving in one direction; it was the inner strength that protected me along the way.

Every morning, as I settled into my desk to face another day, the routine could feel repetitive, like yesterday and the day before. Yet, I understood that the most significant changes often emerge from such repetition. As I inched toward each project's objectives, I quietly nurtured a growing trust in myself. Small, daily resolutions—to make today slightly better than yesterday, to shape tomorrow into something even stronger—added up over time.

In this way, each moment built on the last, bringing about meaningful change and helping me foster self-belief. True achievement didn't stem from raw talent or skill alone. Instead, it began with the accumulation of modest victories, each step forming part of a larger process that gradually completed me.

As I journey forward, I realize that the most essential part of this path isn't in hastily reaching the end but in pacing myself to walk it mindfully, steadily, and with conviction. I trust that by walking each day with intention, the small accomplishments will ultimately come together to yield lasting success, making me stronger and more resilient.

The Fruit of Perseverance: The Joy of Promotion and Achievement

True perseverance eventually led me to the seat of promotion. The new title on my desk was more than a mere label; it was a quiet yet profound acknowledgment of the grit and patience I had accumulated over the years, as well as a small reward for my commitment to moving forward without faltering. With each passing moment, the weight of the path I'd taken sat heavily upon my shoulders, reminding me of my journey and the small but steady achievements left in my wake.

The trust bestowed upon me was not solely the result of my performance. It represented the weight of the confidence my colleagues and mentors placed in me, having watched my progress. In my new position, I felt the responsibility that accompanied their trust. Every step I took, even the small victories, was built upon countless moments of resilience and recovery. The perseverance I held onto through each failure—this was the essence that allowed me to stand in my new role.

The memories of several setbacks lingered vividly. They were never easy moments. I remember the sting of self-doubt and the darkness that often felt insurmountable. Yet, within those trials were small lessons that gradually shaped me into who I am today. My patience and resilience had not been in vain.

In that new seat, I whispered to myself, "Perseverance isn't simply about charging toward a goal; it's about believing in oneself while journeying through unknown paths." My journey was never a solitary one. My colleagues walked with me, lifting me through each failure, their trust woven into every step I took. Their encouragement and faith made me stronger, serving as a quiet yet steadfast force that propelled me forward.

The joy of promotion was more than a personal success—it was a shared achievement with everyone who had supported me along the way. In that moment, I acknowledged the significance of walking this path together. Although the responsibilities of my new role were heavier, I knew that I would continue to walk with the same conviction.

This success was not an end but the beginning of a new chapter.

New Challenges and Fresh Goals

With promotion came another layer of responsibility. The expectations and demands that came with it surrounded me, yet I understood something fundamental. Growth wasn't the result of one grand success but the accumulation of small, consistent achievements. Each day's efforts formed the sturdy steps that would guide me forward.

Standing before a new goal, I felt a mixture of fear and excitement. I knew the road ahead would be demanding, but I trusted that the years of preparation and perseverance would uphold me. The small victories I'd won in the darkness, each added layer of resilience, now illuminated the path ahead like guiding stars, fortifying me for this next journey.

Then, one day, a new realization settled in my heart: perseverance and patience were not just the means to an end; they were the essence of growth itself. They strengthened me and helped me build self-trust. Success was not merely about reaching a destination but about the transformation that occurred within me along the way.

Those small triumphs etched deep in my heart whispered words of reassurance: fears and failures were but passing winds. The lessons learned and strengths gained along the way would sustain me in the days to come. My new goal would undoubtedly test me once more, but I was determined that each step would refine me, making me stronger and more grounded.

With promotion came heavier responsibilities, but within that weight, I found an even clearer sense of purpose. I understood that genuine success transcends personal achievement; it's about crafting something meaningful alongside those who walk the path with me.

Part 6: Habits for Sustainable Success

Chapter 1: Small Habits, Big Changes

Success doesn't start with grand dreams; it begins with the quiet voice of commitment that only I could hear in the stillness of dawn. It's the small yet steadfast resolutions that get me moving each day, guiding my gaze forward. True success grows from these seemingly simple but powerful habits, the building blocks of who I am today. Each morning's plan, each solo practice before a PT or a meeting—these preparations were not just routines but times I spent shaping myself.

My morning routine was more than just organizing the day's tasks; it was a chance to set my direction, to steady myself. Every day, as I sat at my desk, reviewing the day's tasks and opening that first page, I fortified my attitude and mindset. In those moments of quiet reflection, I calmed my inner anxieties and prepared myself for the day ahead.

Moments of Preparation: Planting Roots in the Mind

In the quiet hours spent preparing for PT presentations, I found a time for focus and grounding. Alone in a vast meeting room with spread-out materials, I combed through endless data and statistics, imprinting each figure and phrase into my mind, like cautiously crossing a stone bridge over uncertain waters. Each number and term held my efforts and my hours, and I couldn't let them go lightly.

My voice echoed in the meeting room, but I wasn't rehearsing for others; it was a way to steady myself against inner doubts. I whispered each line, imagining questions that could be asked, answering invisible skeptics before they could speak. I saw each audience member vividly in my mind and anticipated their questions, working out my responses. This wasn't just skill-building; it was a quiet space where I could reconcile my fears and reinforce my resolve.

In the seemingly endless hours of rehearsing and repeating, I grew stronger. Preparation was not about achieving perfection. It was the process of removing self-doubt and creating a foundation of trust in myself. Each solitary practice and every small triumph in my quiet routines built the confidence I would need to face a room without wavering.

Some days were tougher than others. The approaching PT felt like a giant wave threatening to consume me. Yet, I didn't waver. I believed that this preparation would support me, that these repetitions would lead me to safety. Gradually, I understood that fear often springs from insufficient preparation, and these practices showed me how to manage that fear. Although fear never fully disappeared, each moment of preparation taught me how to confront it.

Through this discipline, I gained a fresh perspective. By grounding myself in times of uncertainty, I developed a quiet trust in my own efforts. This trust wasn't about knowing every fact or perfecting every response; it was a belief in my hard work and the hours I'd invested. When my resolve wavered, those countless hours became the seed of confidence I nurtured.

I eventually realized that preparation is not just memorizing scripts or securing flawless answers. It's the foundation within myself. My anxieties subsided, and my steps became lighter. The true gift of my preparation was not perfection or a guarantee of success; it was building a trust in myself and my commitment.

And so, these moments of preparation continued to accumulate until they erected a solid pillar within me—a steadfast center of strength that became my grounding force in the face of any challenge.

Thorough Preparation: My Anchor

Each document I prepared wasn't just filled with numbers and words; it was another way to express myself. Every small figure and chart reflected the time and thought I had invested. Though they seemed like cold, sterile data on the surface, I had put my dedication into them, and that gave me the confidence to stand firm before others. There were moments during PTs and meetings when the weight of the documents in my hand felt heavy, but that weight carried my dedication, allowing me to withstand it with ease. Each line, each figure on the page, was a sincere message I was sending to my audience.

One day, during a critical PT, I was caught off guard by an

unexpected question. For a brief moment, it felt like a dark fog surrounded me. Yet, I realized that I already had the answer within me. That answer lay within the small figures and analysis in my materials. Calmly, I turned the pages, grounding my response in the careful calculations I'd prepared. Each word I spoke was far from improvised; it was the result of diligent preparation, having anticipated their questions and worked through every variable. In that moment, the document was my sturdy support.

Those papers weren't just sheets covered in data. They were a reflection of my commitment and discipline. Without them, I might have faltered under the barrage of questions. But those documents silently supported me, serving as a bridge to communicate my sincerity. Each number and letter wasn't just data—they were my beliefs and intentions, and in that moment, I knew this deeply.

That experience taught me the profound impact of even the smallest preparations. The details I'd devoted to each number and line, every careful consideration—they weren't just information but proof of my resolve. Through my PT and explanations, my audience wasn't merely receiving information; they were seeing my attitude and dedication. Those documents were silent markers of my consistency and readiness, allowing me to present myself openly to others.

Thus, I carved pieces of myself into these ordinary sheets of paper. Night after night, I reviewed those figures and words, building my reasons to remain steadfast. Those documents, filled with countless phrases and numbers, weren't merely data but an honest reflection of me, the most genuine voice I could offer to the world.

The Path Shaped by Small Habits

My strength didn't come from grand leaps, but from small daily habits. Every morning, I took a quiet moment by the window before beginning my day. With a cup of coffee, I would think about my day's goals and reaffirm my resolve. This brief ritual became a wellspring of calm, allowing me to face fears and uncertainties without losing my balance. Like dewdrops gathering to nourish a leaf, these habits gradually strengthened and guided me.

Habits are small and seemingly light, yet they grow in strength over time. Each morning walk, each evening spent at my desk reflecting on the day's events—they were my compass, keeping me grounded. One day, I had a realization: success isn't achieved in a single moment. Rather, it is woven from the accumulation of daily victories, each small accomplishment paving a path beneath my feet. These habits became my source of resilience, steadying me for greater challenges. At last, I felt deeply that the habits I'd cultivated were quietly shaping my journey.

One day, as I looked back on my journey, I realized that every step I had taken had coalesced into a solid foundation. Each habit, accumulated day by day, had given me the strength to keep moving forward without wavering. That path granted me the resilience to stand up after failures and confusion and allowed me to find renewed purpose. In moments of uncertainty, my small habits would lift me, instilling new courage.

Habits may be small, but they become an unshakable force with time. And as I walk this path, I am continually discovering new parts of myself.

Chapter 2: Maintaining Balance Between Work and Life

In professional life, finding a balance between work and personal life is not merely about dividing working hours from personal time. Within any organization, certain roles inherently come with constant responsibilities, sometimes stretching into weekends or late nights. Amid these circumstances, I held on to two key aspects: growth through my work and finding moments of peace within my personal life.

Moments in the Shade: My Father

My father had been battling a chronic lung condition and spent long periods in the hospital. The voice I heard over the phone every few days grew weaker, yet I found myself repeatedly postponing visits, telling myself I was too busy. Then one day, my father gently asked, "Could you come by next week?" His words lingered with me, bearing a quiet hope, possibly a final one. Even then, I only responded, "I'll try to come soon," and hung up the call.

Seasons passed, and my father's health declined rapidly. When I finally saw him in his hospital room, he seemed like a different person, frail and distant. His last words to me, "Alright, let's do that," felt like a soft whisper of goodbye that he didn't have the strength to repeat. As I left his empty room that day, his words stayed with me, guiding me to rethink the meaning of life and the spaces we choose to fill. I realized that my remaining time should be spent on what truly matters. My father's voice, with his gentle reminder, became like a quiet shade, supporting me.

Even now, as I turn off the office lights late at night, thoughts of my father return. Reflecting on all our moments together, I realize that they were like a shade to me, allowing me to rest, to reflect, and to gather strength for the next steps. In the quiet shelter my father left behind, I strive to be a warmer, more thoughtful person. And like him, I wish to be generous with my time, giving freely to those around me. The greatest gift my father left me was the understanding of what true relationships and love mean.

Practicing Balance in the Workplace

Efforts to Balance the Individual and the Team

Pursuing work-life balance within an organization is vital for both personal and team well-being. I encouraged team members to refrain from work-related requests during weekends or after hours, and I streamlined our workflow to allow each person to work efficiently within their role. This approach enabled each team member to feel responsible for their tasks while still preserving balance between work and personal life. As a result, stress and fatigue levels decreased, leading to sharper focus and better performance. Trust within the team grew stronger, reinforcing a positive cycle of mutual support.

In decision-making, I also prioritized collaboration over individual judgment. When differing opinions arose on certain projects, I refrained from unilateral decisions and instead took the time to talk with team members and incorporate their perspectives. This process fostered autonomy and responsibility among team members, reducing their workload stress and helping each person find their own work-life balance. Such balanced structure not only elevated my own performance but also became a source of growth and success for the entire team.

Sustained Growth and Reflection Through Balance

The balance between personal stability and team growth brought deep insights that impacted our organization's long-term success. Work-life balance extended beyond stress relief; it fostered a shift in our organizational culture from being solely results-driven to valuing process-oriented growth. Moments of personal reflection during daily work allowed me to make better decisions and adopt a supportive mindset that encouraged my team to grow alongside me.

As projects unfolded, I realized that focusing solely on successful outcomes was not enough; the sense of fulfillment that team members derived from the journey played a critical role in the organization's long-term development. Achieving balance within a team went beyond setting boundaries for work hours. It involved nurturing trust and open communication, creating an environment where each person could feel valued and experience growth within their role.

One day, after a particularly challenging project had concluded, we held a team meeting to reflect on the journey. I encouraged the team to focus not only on the results but also on the insights and growth they had experienced. A team member shared their story, saying, "This project made me realize how valuable my role is to the bigger picture." In that moment, I understood that work-life balance is not only essential for individual stability but also a cornerstone for our team's collective, long-term progress.

Through the pursuit of balance, I gained more than improved efficiency. I saw that by finding purpose in both work and life, we became a network of support for one another. This balance has since become a guiding principle, shaping the direction and culture we aim to build as an organization.

Chapter 3: Realignment and Growth After Success

When I was granted the title of "success," I knew it did not signify an end. The moment of victory was fleeting, a mere instant. Beyond that brief moment, something even greater awaited me. Standing on this path, I had to ask myself, despite the long, arduous road I'd walked to reach this point, why must I now continue to move forward? The answer was unclear, but I sensed that I had to pursue even higher ground.

Becoming the CEO overseeing an entire group of subsidiaries felt like stepping into an entirely new realm. Everything had changed. On some days, the sheer weight of responsibilities bore down on me; on others, unexpected challenges arose like waves, shaking my carefully laid plans. In those moments, what kept me grounded was the resolve to evaluate myself continually and adapt to meet each new challenge head-on.

Facing a New Beginning, Not an End

At the threshold of success, what awaited me was not only celebration and relief but the weight of greater responsibility and a new, heavier burden. I could no longer be content with the accomplishments of a small team. Back then, each day's progress felt tangible and within reach. But now, overseeing every subsidiary's accomplishments, both big and small, felt like an intricate web resting on my shoulders, and the weight pressed down on me with intensity. Success was the beginning of a new journey, one with even more trials and tests.

I soon realized that the methods I had relied on in the past wouldn't be enough to navigate this evolving landscape. Each step required recalibration. I couldn't linger on minor victories or fixate on small problems; my perspective had to be broader, more far-reaching. I needed to move forward with resilience yet flexibility, aiming higher with each step.

Reading reports every day, visiting sites, and immersing myself in each aspect of the business were not just managerial duties; they were part of a process pulling me toward new horizons. This role demanded that I confront and surpass my limitations daily. There was no room to look back or to rest on past achievements. On the threshold of this new beginning, I kept asking myself questions and seeking answers, continuously realigning my path.

Change did not come swiftly. Often, each step forward felt painstakingly slow, and the resolve required to take that step sometimes felt overwhelmingly heavy. But I knew that this weight was molding me into something stronger. This journey was not only reshaping my actions but also deepening my inner self. These challenges, I realized, were exactly what this position demanded of me.

In my role, responsible for decisions impacting not just a single subsidiary but the entire group, I was transforming each day. At the intersection of success and a new beginning, I constantly reassessed my direction, expanding both my vision and my way of thinking. Though the process was sometimes disorienting, even that chaos served as fuel for growth. The road ahead would not be smooth, but I knew it would not halt my steps.

Each new day on this path could be exhausting, yet it also provided endless inspiration. With each step forward, I believed that my journey would ultimately reveal a deeper purpose. Each small decision and every choice I made brought me closer to my new beginning. I realized that this was an endless journey of growth—my next goal and my path forward.

The Weight of Time Spent Examining Oneself

Each morning, as I settle into my office chair with a steaming cup of coffee, I feel a familiar pull, as though I'm returning to the day I first arrived here. The aroma brings with it weighty questions that surface with the first sip. "What brought me this far? What have I gained along the way, and what have I lost?" Some days, the answers come easily; other days, those questions feel so heavy they unsettle the rhythm of my entire day. Yet I've learned that asking myself these questions every morning is the only way to keep myself grounded, to keep moving forward without losing sight of who I am.

Self-reflection is not merely a retrospective exercise or a confession of past actions. It is a deliberate act of walking forward with eyes wide open, intent on the future. Even now, I tread this path daily, but some days the end goal seems so distant that even a single step feels daunting. On those days, I take a slow sip of coffee, trying to tune in to the quieter voices within. Before beginning each day, I engage in a dialogue with myself, reaffirming my intentions and purpose. This simple act anchors me, helping me stay true to my path, even amid the world's expectations and pressures.

The label of "success" has often pulled me into confusion. At times, I questioned whether the path I followed was a choice or simply the outcome of circumstances pushing me along. Such thoughts would lead me to doubt myself, leaving me in a shroud of unease. But these doubts became seeds for new resolve. To keep those doubts from swaying me, I make a small vow to myself every morning: "Let's move forward steadily today. Let's not forget the purpose that brought me here or the convictions that ground me." This commitment grants me a moment of calm in the quiet of dawn.

In these daily vows, I find myself recalibrating and realigning with my inner direction, searching for the way forward. This path is seldom straightforward. Often, I pause at unexpected crossroads, revisiting choices I thought I had settled. My sense of self might waver in those moments, yet each time I recommit to my journey, I feel myself growing a little stronger. To keep success from becoming a prison, I ask myself each morning who I am, what I am here to achieve, and why I walk this road. I answer, then take another step.

It has been a journey to not lose myself. Success has lifted me, but I vigilantly guard against the risk of it becoming a shackle. Each day,

I erect myself anew with a fresh resolve, knowing that these small daily commitments will ultimately paint the larger canvas of my life. I hold this faith close, trusting that the small steps I take will allow me to continue along this path, unwavering, steady, and true.

Embracing All Changes, Seeking New Paths for Growth

When I was given the responsibility to manage an entire group of affiliates, the challenges I faced tested me in ways I hadn't encountered before. I found myself immersed in a larger, more complex system, tangled with a network of individuals, countless intersecting interests, and multifaceted relationships. It didn't take long to realize that my past achievements and methods would no longer suffice to navigate this new territory. The reality I faced was clear: I had to evolve and, even more, to lead this evolution. This was why I had reached this position and the direction I was now compelled to take.

My past goals had been relatively straightforward and often focused on achieving short-term wins. But this new role demanded a different approach. Each decision I made now held consequences for the company as a whole, far beyond immediate results. I had to envision a future beyond numbers and outcomes—a long-term vision. Instead of reveling in smaller victories, I was now charged with charting a course for the company's future, every step and decision becoming a brushstroke on a canvas much larger than myself. That vision and responsibility were solely mine to bear.

Communication became not just an asset but a necessity. Success was no longer achievable through a single, trusted relationship. Now, it was essential to connect deeply with each affiliate, each team, and the individuals within them. I needed to respect every voice and genuinely listen, engaging in meaningful conversations. Alone, I could achieve nothing; thus, I approached each interaction with a listening ear and an open heart, aiming to foster bonds where growth could flow mutually. I hoped these connections would become the driving force for our shared journey toward a common purpose.

Directing the organization's path required meticulous planning, each step forward deliberate and strategic. Ultimately, every decision landed on my shoulders, and the weight of each outcome came back to me alone. At times, that weight bore down heavily, and a quiet fear would rise from deep within. Yet I did not retreat. Instead, I accepted that weight as mine to carry, an inseparable part of the role of CEO. Each day, I met my responsibilities with the resolve to fully embrace this burden.

Constantly, I asked myself where the future I envisioned would lead this company. This question broadened my perspective, and each step became an exploration of new possibilities. Even when the future seemed uncertain, I looked inward to chart a growth path not just for myself but for the company. I hoped this journey would be one we could walk together, where each step forward would shine a light on shared growth, reflecting back on us all.

Every day, I continue to ask myself, "In the midst of these changes, what must I hold onto? What must I let go of to advance forward?" In answering these questions, I look within and carve out new directions. My growth now reaches beyond individual accomplishments, as I stand on a path that considers a future in which we, as a collective, move forward together.

The Drive to Surpass Oneself, The Need for Constant Growth

One night, standing by the window, I gazed out at the city lights stretching endlessly, lined up like trees on a road. Amidst the scattered lights, a question overwhelmed me: "Where am I headed?" It was a question heavy with significance. It pressed me to examine the weight of the path I'd traveled, the achievements I'd reached, and the meaning of those accomplishments. In the silence of the sleeping city, this place seemed like a stage where I alone was tested. Looking back at what I had achieved did not bring satisfaction. Instead, it brought a sober realization—that there were still places I hadn't yet reached, goals waiting beyond where I stood.

Success, I realized, wasn't merely a destination or a single goal. It wasn't a set of achievements to be measured or an external validation. Rather, success was a continual challenge directed at myself, an ongoing journey to surpass my own limits. I began asking myself: was the road I'd traveled the one I truly desired? What more could I accomplish from this place? What was my next goal? Faced with these questions, I couldn't stop moving forward. On this path, success was never the endpoint. It was a continuous beginning, a call to look within and push onward.

Perhaps I was destined to surpass myself each day—not for the sake of more achievements, but to uncover the potential within me and test myself against greater aspirations. The resolution to go beyond myself had long been growing within me. It urged me to take on deeper responsibility and see from a broader perspective. To fully comprehend the world I was part of and the goals I had yet to reach, I needed to become better than I was today. My success wasn't about standing on past accomplishments, but about finding a path that led beyond them, a path of continuous improvement.

In moments of success, I reaffirmed my beliefs and took each step toward embodying them. Each moment I dedicated to these principles became a part of my growth. On this endless road, I constantly checked my direction, refining my course. The desire to transcend myself served as my compass. Some days, the weight of responsibility and fear threatened to consume me, but I recalled my purpose and summoned my courage. Growth was not an easy journey; it required moments of self-doubt and self-discipline. Yet, it was precisely those difficult times that truly strengthened me.

I no longer questioned why I walked this path. In the pursuit of my goals and beliefs, the purpose became clear on its own. The road ahead was one where I would have to surpass my past self. Greater challenges would surely await, and I needed to be prepared to face them. Growth meant leaping beyond what I'd built so far, continually surpassing myself, and striving toward ever-greater challenges.

At the pinnacle of success, I found myself at a new starting line. Committing all I had to the vision of a better future and aiming higher than ever before, I began again. There was only one reason I could return to the beginning: it was the will to transcend myself and forge new paths toward a broader world.

True Growth Through Daily Reflection

Even after reaching success, the drive that kept me moving forward was within me. It came from the daily habit of self-reflection, rediscovering the potential still lying dormant within, and reigniting it each day. Success wasn't merely an endpoint; it was a new beginning, guiding me toward uncharted destinations. I made sure this success didn't consume me by reorienting myself each day. Success was a message to broaden my perspective, to embrace greater responsibility. While past achievements may validate me, I refused to settle. Each moment of introspection refined me little by little.

Today, once again, I look back on my journey. Those faint traces, small mistakes I once overlooked from the summit of success, have now become engraved on each page of my life, guiding me to better places. My past shortcomings, the doubts I wrestled with, shaped who I am today and serve as valuable markers for my future. I no longer take time for granted. To truly carry the weight of "success" means not only to honor my potential but to continually assess and nurture it.

As I pause each day to evaluate my steps, I discover new seeds of possibility still waiting to blossom. I hope these seeds will grow into towering trees along my path, and I am resolved to take yet another step forward tomorrow.

The chapters of my story yet to unfold, and the goals I have yet to reach, are what propel me forward. The joy of success is fleeting, while the responsibility and weight it carries remain with me far longer. Yet, it's this very weight that fuels my strength to press on. Without it, perhaps I would have lost the reason to look toward higher places.

So today, I carve in my heart the path I've taken and the road that lies ahead, rising once again. The time that has shaped me, and the weight it left behind, will continue to push me forward. At the intersection where my past meets my present, I am crafting a new self. Each day becomes a new beginning, a chance for further growth. The road I've walked propels me onward. Knowing this journey will never truly end, I brace myself, building resilience within, and take my next step toward tomorrow.

Epilogue: Walking Together on an Endless Journey of Growth

One day, I realized my journey was no longer a solitary one. With each step forward, I noticed those walking alongside me, reaching out a hand, or at times, taking hold of the hand I extended to them. In different roles yet on the same path, we moved toward our individual goals, and together we embraced something larger.

As CEO, prioritizing the well-being of our employees and customers became my primary duty—made possible because of those by my side. Without their trust and support, I would not be standing here today. I learned that the greatest value lies in shared growth, where the journey of "becoming" isn't mine alone, but the product of countless efforts moving forward, even in this very moment. Though we stand in different places, we look to the same horizon, driven by a shared vision—a vision that transcends mere profit or performance metrics. It is a dream of a future we want to build together, one that holds the essence of a better world, for each of us and for all of us.

Every day, as I walk through our office doors, I picture the faces of those who give life to this company—the ones dreaming beside me and transforming those dreams into reality. Their presence fuels my desire to make better choices and take us in the right direction, as I think about what my decisions mean in their lives and what kind of future we are creating together. In this way, we become meaningful parts of each other's journeys.

A Journey Walked Together

Being CEO taught me countless lessons. I realized that true success does not lie in walking alone or deciding everything by oneself. Real success lies in moving forward on a path where we can grow alongside one another, supporting each other along the way. Every day, I witness our employees giving their all, standing firm in their roles, while the trust of customers choosing us out of loyalty and affection continually renews my inspiration.

Some days were tough. Bearing the weight of countless decisions, knowing each one allowed no room for error, sometimes wore me down. Yet, even in those moments, I could not stop. Behind me stood people committed to walking this journey with me. They were my guiding light, my reason. Because of them, I found strength to endure each moment, and they became my partners along this path, just as I hoped to become a source of support for them. Together, leaning on each other, we were able to ascend a little higher, one step at a time.

A Heartfelt Dedication to Those Who Walked Alongside Me

In this endless journey of growth, we shared our dedication and passion. My achievements became theirs, and their successes filled me with joy. The sweat and hard work each of us invested became precious assets, fueling a future for this company, for them, and for me. We continually strove to do our best for one another, and this commitment became the foundation of our mutual growth.

As I look back on each moment shared, I recall the conversations with colleagues, the promises to our clients, and the hours we poured into making our dreams a reality. Those who believed in my path and placed their trust in me are the very reason I stand here today. Their faith is never taken lightly. That trust has nurtured this company, and it continues to propel me forward, lighting the way on this journey without end.

Reflecting on the Meaning of Growth

I have come to realize that true growth is not about individual success, but about creating a path that embraces us all. For the success of us, not just me, I am committed once again to giving my best from where I stand. I believe that our shared growth is the foundation of a better future, and with that in mind, I will strive to shape a new tomorrow alongside everyone who walks this journey with me. They are my purpose and my strength. Their presence is more than just a reminder of success; it is the very reason behind every endeavor I undertake.

This journey will continue, as it always has, with us standing side by side, lending each other trust and support. Their growth will be my joy. The most profound realization I've gained while leading this company is that true success is not in my growth alone, but in the shared growth of all. Every decision I make, every step I take from here on, will be with them in mind—so they can dream even bigger and walk alongside me towards those dreams.

To all those who have walked this long journey hand in hand with me, I extend my deepest gratitude. They have been my strength, my light, and my journey.

To Everyone Reading This Book

As you embark on this new journey of life, know that countless paths, some yet unseen, stretch out before you. There will be times when you stand at a crossroads of choices, or find yourself alone in the darkness, with no clear path in sight. Taking the first step into the professional world is a journey that combines excitement with a vague sense of fear. But remember, no matter how vast and complex the world may seem, keep your belief in yourself close. Trust in yourself, and learn to listen to your inner voice, for that is what will keep you steadfast on any path you may encounter.

As we part, there are five lessons I hope to leave with you.

First, believe in yourself.
What you possess may not yet be fully known to the world. There may be times when you feel unsure or even doubt yourself, not yet aware of the full extent of your own abilities. But hold firm to your self-belief. The world may test you, and others may try to measure your worth through evaluations or judgments. Each time that happens, nurture a strong and steady belief within. Though it may seem small now, that belief will be the foundation of your journey. Have faith in yourself and move forward.

Second, do not fear failure.
Failure may bring discomfort, but it is life's most powerful teacher. Although failure can feel intimidating, it ultimately deepens and

strengthens us. Learn from your setbacks, and search for better paths forward; this is what will ultimately open the door to success. The insights gained from failure will serve as a guiding light on your journey, a gift that is more precious than any success.

Third, don't overlook even the smallest tasks.
Sometimes, the tasks that seem insignificant can leave the most lasting impact on your growth. These achievements may feel small at the moment, but over time they will build up to form your own history. The steady accumulation of effort and small successes day by day will become your career's foundation and provide fertile ground for greater opportunities. For those who devote genuine effort to the small things, the doors to greater opportunities will eventually open.

Fourth, cherish relationships.
The people you meet in your professional life are not simply coworkers or clients; they are sources of inspiration and opportunities for mutual growth. Build trust and listen deeply to their stories. When you truly understand and empathize with others, growth arises within those relationships. The sincerity you give will one day return to you, and the shared achievements rooted in trust will be far more rewarding and enduring than any that you achieve alone.

Lastly, pace yourself and keep moving forward.
There will be moments when the path ahead feels obscured. During such times, care for yourself, take a rest, and gather your strength

anew. Pausing is not a step backward; it is a necessary preparation to continue moving forward. In the end, you will rise and find the strength to press on.

For every step you take on this journey, know that the power you need resides within. Carry that inner strength as you go, and may it light your way to the success and growth you seek.

Difficulties and setbacks are inevitable parts of life. Failure isn't just a process to be endured—it is one of life's most powerful teachers. At times, mistakes may lead you to self-doubt or regret, yet believe that these moments will shape you into a stronger, deeper person. Learn from failure, cultivate the resilience to pick yourself up, and develop the strength to persevere. Failure is not an end but a necessary interval for realignment and fortification, guiding you toward a brighter future.

In your professional life, remember that even small, seemingly trivial tasks accumulate to create substantial change. These minor achievements may initially feel insignificant, but each one will serve as a building block in the foundation of your career. Approach each day's work with diligence, giving your best effort. You're not just creating ripples—you're preparing for the waves that will one day propel you forward. Those waves, in turn, will converge into a great current that opens the path to your success.

Cherish the relationships you form along this journey. The people you work with are not mere colleagues; they are companions and teachers who contribute to your growth. As you navigate these relationships, you'll find that genuine listening and empathy are key. Listening with sincerity, connecting with others in their joy and struggles—these are the foundations upon which true trust is built. Shared successes bring deeper joy and growth than any solitary accomplishment ever could. The trust and friendships you forge will become invaluable assets throughout the long path of life.

Above all, do not forget the importance of self-care on this journey. In the pursuit of success, it can be all too easy to push yourself past your limits. While the urge to keep moving forward without pause may arise, sometimes allowing yourself time to rest and realign is the most powerful strategy for sustainable progress. In moments of loneliness or overwhelm, pause to care for yourself. Acknowledge your efforts, offer yourself words of encouragement, and honor your achievements—however small they may seem. You'll find renewed strength and courage to continue.

The world may sometimes seem daunting, but you are already prepared to undertake this journey. Amid hardship and uncertainty, trust in yourself, and you will inevitably find your way to brighter paths. The efforts and sincerity you invest today will someday be the bedrock that supports you. When you look back, you will see how far you've come, standing upon a foundation you built with resolve and heart.

A Realization Found in Conversations with Myself: On My Final Walk from Work

On my last walk from work, I paused, unexpectedly, just as I was stepping out of the office. Gazing through the windows at the end of the long corridor, the cityscape beyond felt somehow different, gently casting a quiet resonance over me, pulling me into reflection on the path I'd walked to reach this moment.

The chill of the evening air brushed my face, and memories of my first day flooded back: the mingled fear and anticipation, the thrill of beginnings, the weight of countless projects, the rhythm of repeated failures, and the steady resolve to try once more. As I walked, I found myself in silent conversation, asking, "Where am I now? What have I gained from all of this?" Slowly, it felt as though an answer began to form, emerging softly from somewhere deep within me.

Looking up at the sky, sprinkled with the lights of the city, I found myself recognizing the true gifts this journey had left me. It wasn't about visible accomplishments alone. It was the resilience I'd forged by falling and rising again, the trust built through earnest connection with others, and above all, the unshakeable belief in myself that had carried me through every moment. I understood that this was never just my journey; it was a shared path, walked with those who stood by me, whose companionship had strengthened my steps. What I held at the end of this path was not a simple notion of success, but the courage that had lifted me time and again.

Standing at this threshold, I felt warmth welling up inside. The day's end was not merely the end of another day; it was a new beginning. The questions I had asked myself, the quiet answers I'd found, would continue to guide me forward. Under the last fading light of the night sky, I closed this long, intimate conversation with myself, softly whispering, "I am grateful for having walked this path, and for the strength to keep walking it onward."

May your own journey be both beautiful and deeply meaningful.

On a beautiful November day in 2024, just before the full cold settles

SEONG OUK JUNG

www.ingramcontent.com/pod-product-compliance
Lightning Source LLC
Chambersburg PA
CBHW052356220526
45465CB00003BB/1127